T0118950

Knit, Hook, and Spin

A Kid's Activity Guide to
Fiber Arts and Crafts

Laurie Carlson

CHICAGO
REVIEW
PRESS

Copyright © 2016 by Laurie Carlson
All rights reserved
Published by Chicago Review Press Incorporated
814 North Franklin Street
Chicago, Illinois 60610

ISBN 978-1-61373-400-1

Library of Congress Cataloging-in-Publication Data
Names: Carlson, Laurie M., 1952– author.
Title: Knit, hook, and spin : a kid's activity guide to fiber arts and crafts
 / Laurie Carlson.
Description: Chicago, Illinois : Chicago Review Press Incorporated, [2016] |
 Audience: Age: 9+.-
Identifiers: LCCN 2015044783 | ISBN 9781613734001 (trade paper)
Subjects: LCSH: Textile crafts—Juvenile literature.
Classification: LCC TT712 .C37 2016 | DDC 745.5—dc23 LC record
available at http://lccn.loc.gov/2015044783

Cover design: Jonathan Hahn
Interior design: Sarah Olson
Cover and interior illustrations: Jim Spence

Printed in the United States of America
5 4 3 2 1

Contents

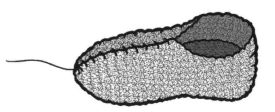

Introduction

Welcome to the wonderful world of fiber arts and crafts! People have been making things with fiber for thousands of years. Using fibers from animal hair or pieces of plants, people could make fishing lines and nets, blankets, tents, and clothing, allowing them to stay fed, warm, and sheltered.

Today, when machines seem to do everything for us, we don't have to create everything we wear or use. We can buy things we need. But millions of people still work with fiber because they enjoy making things with their hands. In fact, fiber arts and crafts are just as popular now as they ever were. At least 50 million people in the United States know how to knit and crochet.

What is "fiber art," anyway? Fiber art is any art form that uses yarn or cloth or the fibers used tomake them. Because fabric and yarn are used so much in everyday clothing and household items, we tend to think of them as simply useful. In fact, they can also be used to make art. Every item made of fabric and yarn was designed by someone. That person decided on the color, texture, and pattern, as well as the shape of the finished item.

When you work with fiber you use a lot of different skills. Math is important, because you'll be measuring length, making patterns of odds and evens, working with geometry and shape, and thinking about amounts, such as more, less, and equal. You'll also work with counting, and comparing top and bottom, in and out, over and under, above and below, and front and back. Whew! It sounds complicated, but it is easy and fun.

Here are a few tips for enjoying your fiber arts adventure:

❧ Choose simple projects that don't take a long time to finish.

❧ Collect yarn, cloth scraps, felt, and fiber stuff in a variety of colors and store them in a box so you have a stash to create with.

❧ Don't expect that your projects will be perfect every time. If something doesn't please you, change it, unravel it, or take it apart and try something else.

❧ Enjoy the items you make. Wear the things you make. Display them in your room. Give them to people you care about.

Why Fiber Handcrafts Are Good for You

You may not think that making things with yarn or fiber would make you smarter or keep you healthy, but it can. Working with fibers and yarn feels good to our sense of touch, and the colors and patterns please the eye. Our senses are sharpened, and that makes us feel happier. Doing handwork, like knitting or crocheting, helps us relax. It also helps us focus and pay attention better. Because following written directions stretches our brain, it's good for our thinking skills. And you can also make changes to a project that make it your own, expressing your creativity.

Some people find that knitting or crocheting helps when they are ill or in pain. Some find that it helps them sleep better at night. Handcrafts take time and attention, so we learn to be more patient and less restless. You'll also figure out how to solve problems when something doesn't seem to be turning out as you thought it would. But best of all, when you are finished with a project, you have a feeling of pride. And lots of gifts to give your friends.

Know Your Fibers

Fiber is the basic ingredient in crafting—sort of like flour for a baker and soil for a gardener. Fibers are thin strands of plant stems (linen), fluff from seed pods (cotton), animal hair (wool), or tiny strands of plastic (acrylic) that are twisted together to make yarn. Fiber can be as thin as sewing thread or as thick as rope. But before fibers can be twisted together, a lot of preparation must be done. Fibers from plants or animals must be clipped, washed, fluffed, combed, and dyed.

Fibers create different types of finished projects. Whether your project will be silky, soft, stretchy, shiny, or warm is determined by the type of fiber. Some fibers can be scratchy—like jute—and are best for ropes or sacks. Do you want something soft and luxurious? Use angora rabbit. Shiny? Well, that's silk or mohair. Washable and nonallergenic? Try synthetics. Warm and fireproof? That's a job for wool. The more you know about fibers, the easier it will be for you to match the right fiber to your project.

Plant Fibers

People used plant fibers long before they discovered any of the others. They plucked grassy stems, strips of stringy tree bark, and long skinny leaves from the natural world around them. They did things to the pieces of bark or leaves to make them easier to bend and shape to suit what they wanted to make. They were processing the fiber, making it both easier to work with and longer lasting once a project was complete.

From those plant fibers, people made nets and ropes that made it easier to catch fish, birds, and small animals for food. They made mats that they used as roofing on their homes and for sleeping pads. Listed here are the plants most commonly used in fiber and fabric today.

COTTON

Cotton is a fluffy fiber that comes from the boll, or flower, of the cotton plant. It was grown in Egypt, Asia, and South America for 6,000 years. It was grown by Native Americans in North America and became a valuable farming product in the southern United States about 200 years ago. Northern Europeans relied on sheep's wool, because cotton plants didn't grow well in their cold climate. People there called cotton "tree wool," because the fluffy puffs of fiber looked like pieces of sheep's wool stuck on a branch.

FLAX (LINEN)

The fibers of the flax plant are used to make a fabric called linen. It is a lot of work to get flax ready to spin. The full-grown plant is pulled from the earth, with the roots hanging. Then a rough comb is pulled through the stem to remove the seeds. The stem part is soaked in water for a few weeks until it begins to rot. Then it is dried in the sun. Next, the flax stems are beaten against a board and combed with metal combs. Finally, the strands can be separated from each other and spun into linen thread, ready for knitting or weaving.

Flax plants grow best in colder, wetter climates, such as northern Europe and Canada—places where cotton doesn't grow well.

HEMP

Hemp plants have been grown for their fiber for about 10,000 years. Hemp plants are processed like flax. It is a rough but strong fiber that was used for fabric and ship sails in the past but is mostly used to make cord, rope, and sacks today. Synthetic fibers have replaced most hemp use around the world.

JUTE

Jute plants grow in wet, warm areas with warm rains. Most jute is grown in India and Bangladesh. Jute plants don't need fertilizer or insect spray, and jute fiber is completely biodegradable. Jute is used to make twine, rope, and sacks. Jute sacks were very commonly used in the past for holding wheat, beans, and other farm products. Today those sacks are made of plastic. Jute strings are used as a backing for making carpeting, but plastic is replacing it for that purpose, too.

SOYBEANS

Soybeans are pressed and treated to make a yarn that is soft like silk. Soybean plants are field crops grown in many parts of the world today.

BAMBOO

Bamboo yarn is made from the cellulose (fiber) in the bamboo stalk. Bamboo grows in wet tropical climates.

CORN

Starches in corn are turned into sugars, fermented, and then separated into a paste that is pushed out a machine with tiny holes called a spinneret, making delicate strands. Corn yarn feels a lot like cotton yarn, but it melts very easily if it is ironed. It hasn't become popular yet.

Animal Fibers

No one really knows when people began to use animal hair to make string, rope, and fabric. People used animal hides and skins for most of their clothing and bedding for a long time. Because hair rots away easily, very little has been found in archaeological remains. Below are some of the most common fibers made from animal hair. In addition to the animals and insects mentioned below, hair from alpacas, camels, llamas, possums, and yaks can be used to make fiber.

WOOL

Wool, made from the hair from sheep, was probably the first fiber people used, because they could easily gather it where it snagged on branches or fell on the ground. That's because sheep used to shed their hair every spring, so for thousands of years, people just walked around and gathered up wool where they could find it. Wool gathering was done by children as they watched over the grazing flocks. They would sometimes spin the wool into yarn right in the pasture using a hand spindle. Over the centuries, metalworking was developed and shears were invented. That meant farmers began to select sheep that didn't drop their hair, and raised them instead of those that shed. That's because it was easier to gather all the wool at one time, when the shearing was done.

Today, sheep are shorn twice a year, in spring and fall. It doesn't hurt them; in fact, having the large mass of thick hair taken off means they can run and move better. It's like getting a haircut over their whole body. Shearing also keeps fleas and lice from making a home on their skin. The hair that is cut off is called fleece.

The fleece is covered with a natural body oil called lanolin, which keeps water from wetting the hair. Sheep can graze comfortably in the rain because the lanolin coating on their hair keeps their skin dry. In the past, fishermen's sweaters were made from unwashed wool and were never laundered. The natural lanolin coating on the yarn made the sweaters waterproof and kept men dry during storms at sea. Some said it helped the sweater float, like a life preserver, if the man fell overboard. Wool is washed today, and the lanolin that is removed is used in making hand cream, soap, hair conditioners, and many other items. Check the labels on your products and you'll probably see that you've been using sheep's lanolin, a by-product from the wool industry.

Wool hairs have tiny scales on their sides that open up like little umbrellas. They also help keep the sheep dry during rainstorms. When wool fiber gets wet, the fibers swell, and the ends of the scales push out and open up. If the wet fibers are pressed and rubbed together the open scales get tangled and the fibers stick together. The matted material is then called felt. If you use hot water and add soap, the scales open up and slide together. They link together,

and when you add pressure or rub the fibers, they lock together and won't come apart.

Plant fibers don't have scales, so they don't mat to make felt. Synthetic felt—which is sold in craft stores—is made by pressing and heating petroleum-based fiber, such as polyester. Synthetic felt won't unravel, but it also won't shrink or mold into shape like wool felt.

MOHAIR

Mohair comes from mohair goats, also called Angora goats. They are a special breed of goat that are nearly completely covered in long curly hair that brushes the ground. They originated in Turkey. Today most mohair goats are raised in South Africa and Texas. Mohair is shiny, soft, and warmer and stronger than wool.

CASHMERE

Cashmere comes from cashmere goats. A cashmere hair is very fine—only one-third as thick as a human hair. It is very soft. Cashmere goats aren't sheared; their hair is combed off the animal by hand. Some hairs are short and some are long, and combing it off helps separate the hairs. Cashmere goats originated in the Himalaya mountains of today's northern India.

Today most cashmere goats are raised in Mongolia and China.

ANGORA

Angora is the very delicate and soft fiber that is combed off special rabbits. Angora fiber is eight times warmer than wool. It can keep you warm even when it's wet. An Angora rabbit produces about eight ounces of fiber a year. That much fiber weighs about the same as two cubes of butter. It is very light and fluffy, however, so that small amount is enough to make a woman's sweater.

SILK

Silk farming started about 4,600 years ago in China. It was a very secret and profitable industry for China for centuries. Silk is made from fibroin, which is made of digested leaves that the silkworm eats then spits out. Farmed silkworms eat only mulberry tree leaves. They make silk fiber that is pure white, called Bombyx silk. Wild silkworms eat cherry leaves, oak leaves, or mulberry leaves, and their silk is darker, from ivory to light brown. It's called Tussah silk.

Silkworms are caterpillars that eat leaves constantly for 30 days, growing 10,000 times their hatchling size. Then the caterpillar finally stops eating and begins spinning its cocoon. It spits out the fibroin as it rotates its body about 200,000 times, ending up wrapped in 800 yards of fibroin thread. The completed cocoon is about the size of a peanut shell.

Silk farmers gather the cocoons and boil them to prevent the moth from developing inside. Then the silk fiber is pulled out of the cocoon in a long continuous thread and wound on a bobbin. Silk is one of the strongest fibers on the planet.

Yes, you could say that silk—one of the finest fibers—is made of worm spit. Check the website www.wormspit.com for more information about silkworms.

For thousands of years the Chinese government wouldn't sell silkworms or eggs to outsiders, only cloth or yarn. Eventually some silkworm eggs and mulberry tree seeds were smuggled to India, hidden in a Chinese princess's headdress. Two centuries later, Persian missionaries smuggled silkworm eggs hidden in walking canes from China to the Roman Empire. Eventually, everyone figured out how silk was made. But it's so much work and the silkworms can only be fed mulberry leaves, so it didn't take hold in very many new areas. There are wild silk moths in some forested areas, such as the Pacific Northwest in the United States, but no industry has developed there.

Man-Made Fibers

RAYON

Rayon was the first fiber created in a laboratory. It is made from cellulose, which is found in wood pulp made from ground-up trees. It is dissolved with chemicals, then squirted through a spinneret. It comes out as a thread, or filament. Rayon threads are spun or woven to make clothing, as well as used to reinforce the rubber in automobile tires. Today, most rayon fiber is made in large factories in India.

SYNTHETIC FIBERS

Synthetic fibers include acrylic, polyester, and nylon. They are made from small molecules of chemicals found in petroleum: petrochemicals. They are made by a process called melt-spinning. The liquid petrochemical mix is heated, then pushed through a spinneret's tiny holes. It comes out in strings of hot plastic syrup. It hardens as it cools. These plastic threads can then be knitted or woven to create fabric or carpet. Today most synthetic fiber is manufactured in Southeast Asia and China.

There are many new fibers being created now; in fact, they are being invented at an astonishing rate. Some are made of recycled materials, such as plastic bottles, blue jeans, or old pieces of clothing. Some are made from natural materials, such as tofu liquid, banana plants, milk, sugar cane stalks, and seaweed. Others are synthetics that glow in the dark or even emit music. Expect more new fibers in the future. Maybe *you* will invent a new fiber, or create one from something ordinary!

THE FIRST FABRIC
Felting

Because you can make felt without any equipment, such as a loom, it was the first fabric people invented. For about 8,000 years people have been making felt with wool because it is so simple to make and can be used in many ways.

Felt has air trapped between the fibers, which makes it a good insulator for heat and cold. It also absorbs sound, so it is used in musical instruments, such as drum sticks, pianos, and xylophones. Felt wicks (absorbs) moisture, and doesn't dry out fast, making it perfect for creating ink markers, or felt pens.

Today, synthetic felt is made from petroleum-based fibers that are pressed and melted together with heat and pressure. It is commonly found in craft stores. Felted synthetic fibers are also found in other items, such as disposable diapers and tea bags. Many things that used to be made of felt are now made from plastics and foam.

You can make your own felt from wool. Use *wool roving* from a yarn store, or 100 percent wool yarn. Wool roving is wool fleece that has been washed and

Yurt houses in Central Asia were traditionally made of wooden poles covered with layers of felt. The houses lasted five to ten years; then new ones were made. A yurt took all the wool from up to 190 sheep. The size of a family's yurt depended on the size of its flock—which determined the amount of wool they had to use.

combed. It can be natural colors or dyed. If you want to felt yarn, be sure it is all wool and contains no synthetic fiber, such as acrylic. If the wool yarn is called superwash it has been treated with chemicals to keep the natural scales from opening, so it can be laundered in a washing machine without felting. That means it won't make felt for you, either. Another good source for wool to use in craft projects is from discarded clothing. An old wool sweater can be unraveled to make lots of projects. Check secondhand and thrift shops for wool sweaters.

Roving is sometimes also sold as carded wool fiber. *Carded* means it has been brushed until the hairs run mostly in one direction.

Felting wool requires hot water, soap, and rubbing (friction).

Felted Soap

People have covered bars of soap with felt since the Middle Ages. The wool felt covering makes a bar of soap last longer, and it also takes the place of a washcloth. Felt-covered soap is a natural scrubber that everyone can enjoy, and it takes very little effort to make.

Materials

2–3 handfuls of carded wool
   fiber or roving
Basin of hot water
Bar of soap
Leg cut from a nylon stocking
Hand towel

❖ Pull the wool fiber apart into strips about 1 inch wide. Wet the fiber and wrap the soap bar completely, overlapping the wool strips to make sure the entire soap is covered.

   Use thin layers of wool. If it gets too thick you may get wrinkles and folds, and those areas won't felt easily.

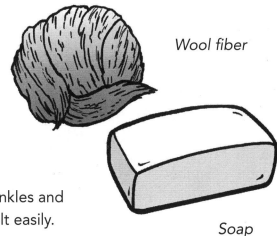

Wool fiber

Soap

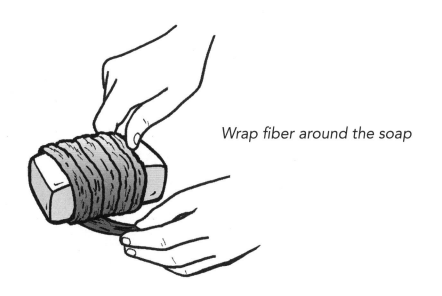

Wrap fiber around the soap

Smooth the wool over the soap and slip it into the toe of the nylon stocking. Hold the stocking and dip the wool-covered bar into the hot water. The heat will open the scales on the wool.

Lift the stocking out of the water, and begin working the wool with your fingers, pressing firmly and rubbing to push the felt scales onto each other. The fibers will tangle and eventually create a solid mass—felt.

Slip soap into a stocking and dip in hot water. Begin rubbing the wool.

Keep working the surface with your fingers, but be careful to not push the wool off the soap. The wool will eventually shrink up due to the pressure and movement of your hands, as the fibers interlock. It will take about five minutes of rubbing in the stocking and two or more dips in the hot water before the fibers stick together completely and blend into a solid layer of felt. If you have trouble getting enough pressure, you can rub the soap back and forth on a baking rack, just like an old-time washboard. Rubbing the wool-covered soap on a piece of plastic bubble wrap can work, too.

Gently pull the stocking off the felted bar. Blot the excess water

and suds off the bar with a dry towel. Let the felted soap dry at least overnight. In a hurry? You can speed up the drying by placing the bar in the sun, over a floor heat vent, or in a food dehydrator or by using a hair dryer.

To make more colorful soaps, you can mix different colors of wool, or wrap different-colored strips over each other, making a marbled look.

Try various colors of wool

Legend has it that Noah padded the floors of his ark with wool, and after 40 days of animals' feet and moisture, it became a mat of felt. Others say travelers lined their shoes with sheep's wool, and after days of walking, the pressure and sweat created felt.

Felted Beads

You can make colorful, soft beads for a necklace from small bits of wool. String them on a length of yarn and add wooden or plastic beads between the felt beads to make it more interesting and colorful.

Materials

Wool roving or carded fleece (see the section on Dyeing to color white wool)
Hot water
Dish or hand soap
Tapestry or yarn needle
Yarn (about a yard)

♣ Working at a sink is easiest, but you can do this activity almost anywhere with a basin of hot water.

Tear bits of wool into chunks about the size of a golf ball. Wet a wool chunk and rub a bit of soap into it. Roll the wool into a ball and continue rubbing it between the palms of your hands. Dip it into hot water and continue rubbing and rolling. You will need to rub and dip a few times to get the fibers to link together. Continue

the process until felting occurs. It will eventually shrink and tighten into a ball.

Repeat this process to make several balls. Set out your felted beads to dry. When they are fully dry, usually about 12 to 24 hours, use a needle threaded with yarn to string them together.

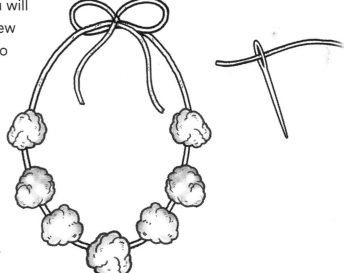

String the felted beads with yarn and a needle. Tie securely to make a necklace.

Felted Balls

You can make felt items by using hot water and soap, and rubbing wool with your hands, but you can also create felted projects by letting the washing machine do most of the work. If you put an item made of pure wool into the washer, using hot water, it will shrink and felt. This would be terrible for your favorite sweater, but if you plan ahead and make a project with the goal of shrinking and felting, it can work very well.

Felt balls are like bigger versions of the beads you made in the previous project. They are really easy to make and can be used in several ways. Use them in games, as holiday tree decorations, as heads for cloth dolls, or give them as gifts. Felt balls can save energy, too. You can put them in the dryer with wet clothing and they will shorten the drying time. Wool wicks moisture, so the balls absorb some of the wetness from the clothing, helping the load dry faster—and using less energy. It's best to use three or more balls in a dryer load.

Roll wool fiber into balls

Materials

Wool, carded as roving or batting, or 100 percent wool yarn (Do not use yarn that can be machine washed—superwash yarn—as it has been treated with chemicals to keep it from felting.) Old wool sweaters can be a good source for yarn. Scraps of yarn work, too. The colors and sizes don't have to match, but they must be wool.
Leg cut from a nylon stocking
Washing machine
Dryer (optional)

❧ Wad a few handfuls of wool to make a ball, adding more wool to make a bigger ball. It's easy to also use yarn, wrapping it tightly around the loose wool to create a round shape, then adding more wool over the yarn to cover it completely. Because the ball will shrink during the felting process, make it a bit larger than you want the finished ball to be.

Slip a ball into the toe of a leg cut from pantyhose. Pull the hose up tightly and knot it above the ball. Make another ball, and tie it in place next to the first one. Add a third ball, too.

With the wool balls securely tied inside the nylon stocking, launder them in a washing machine along with a pair of jeans. Use detergent and the hot water wash setting. The heat and soap will open the wool fibers' scales, and the jeans will agitate the wool balls—all the steps needed to create felt.

When the wash cycle is complete, gently pull the nylon stocking away from the wool balls, and they should be felted. If they aren't felted enough, wash them again inside another nylon stocking leg. You can dry them with a load of wet clothing in the clothes dryer or let them air dry. Check to be sure the wool doesn't felt into the nylon stocking, or it will be difficult to peel the nylon off.

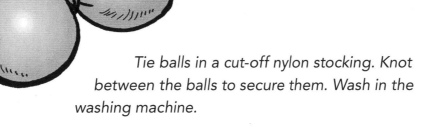

Tie balls in a cut-off nylon stocking. Knot between the balls to secure them. Wash in the washing machine.

Felted Rainbow

You can make sheets of felt in a plastic bag using wool, hot water, soap, and your hands. Try a little rainbow project first, then move to a larger project, the Felt Bag.

Materials

A handful of wool roving in rainbow colors: red, yellow, blue, and white for clouds

Plastic ziplock sandwich bag

1 cup hot water

1 teaspoon liquid dish detergent

✿ Arrange strips of wool to create a rainbow, with clouds at each end. Gently slide the rainbow into a sandwich bag.

Layer colored wool to make a rainbow

Slip the rainbow into a sandwich bag

Combine a cup of hot water and a teaspoon of liquid dish soap, and pour the hot soapy water into the bag to wet the wool completely. Lay the bag flat on a hard surface and begin rubbing

the bag of wool with your fingers and knuckles.

Lay the bag down and press out the water

Squeeze excess water out of the bag as you work. Continue rubbing until the wool is felted together.

Rub the bag of wet wool firmly until it felts

Slip the rainbow out and let it dry flat.

Remove from the bag; let dry flat

Felted Bag

Here's a simple, useful project to try with your felt-making skills. You can use felt pieces alone for kitchen hot pads or decorative wall hangings, but it's really easy to fold felt into bags, pouches, or slipcases for money, phones, or eyeglasses. Add buttons, snaps, or ties if you like.

Materials

1-gallon ziplock plastic bag
Scraps and bits of wool roving or carded wool
Measuring cup
Hot water
Spoon
Liquid dishwashing detergent
Cold water
Towel
Scissors
Tapestry or yarn needle (with a head large enough for yarn)
Yarn

♣ This project is easiest if you work near a sink. You can also move the work area outdoors, with a large pan, hot water in a Thermos, and a tabletop to work on.

Lay the plastic bag flat on the tabletop. Place pieces of wool roving evenly inside the bag, layering them so all of the bag is covered. It should be a thin layer, with no plastic bag showing through, but without thick bumps. Pull the wool apart, then push it into the corners of the bag. Close the bag and hold it up so you can see if any areas need more wool to cover.

Mix a cup of hot water and a spoonful of liquid dishwashing detergent. Lay the bag flat and carefully pour in the soapy water. Begin pressing on the bag of wool to push the water through the wool, squeezing excess water out of the bag.

Rearrange the wool if you need to. Then begin rubbing and pounding the bag of wool with your hands or the back of the spoon, keeping it flat on the table-top. Turn the bag over and do the back side, too. From time to time, pour out the cooled water and add hot water to continue the felting process.

The soap, hot water, and pressure from your hands will create felt. When the pieces are all stuck together, it is felted. Gently slide it out of the bag and dip in cold water. Roll it up in a towel and squeeze gently. Lay it flat to dry.

When the felt is dry, trim the edges evenly with scissors. Fold it in half to make a bag, pouch, or case. Use a needle and yarn to sew up two sides. Sew the edge in a blanket stitch by inserting the needle through the felt and the stitch, as shown, for a nice finished edge.

← *Fold*

Fold

The oldest known felt hats were worn by early Celts—they were a beret style. In ancient Rome, wearing a felt cap meant you had been granted freedom from slavery. In the 1800s, machines made felt hats cheaply; they became very popular for men. Top hats were popular among the wealthy, and bowler hats were worn by most everyone in the city. Cowboy hats were worn out West.

Felt hat styles from yesterday and today

Beret

top hat

bowler hat

cowboy hat

jester cap

mouse ears cap

ALL TIED UP
Knotting and Braiding

Between 20,000 and 30,000 years ago, a remarkable thing happened: the string revolution. People learned to make cord or thread. We don't know when string was invented, but it gave people better ways to survive. It could be knotted to make snares, fishing line, tethers, leashes, and nets. Some people think the invention of string was so powerful that it allowed people to move and settle around the globe during the Stone Age. It could be made easily from wild plant materials long before people decided to plant crops. Later, when groups of people began to live in small villages, they invented pottery.

Cordage refers to rope, twine, or string. It's easy to make some cordage from plant fiber. People have been doing it since the Stone Age—and you can still buy cordage made from plants today. Twine is sold for wrapping packages and for crafts. String made of cotton (a plant) is widely available. You can make twine or lightweight rope from plants such as cattails, milkweed, dogbane, straw, and the inner bark of trees such as willow, pine, fir, and cedar.

Rope bridges are found around the world. In New Guinea, Ireland, the Himalayas, and the Andes, people made bridges from twisted plant fibers. Many are still being used today. Ropes for those bridges are sometimes as thick as an adult's body. The heavy twisted fiber ropes are strong, but eventually they begin to sag. They have to be repaired and rebuilt nearly every year. The entire community comes together to get the work done.

Braided Bracelet

This is the simplest braid-ing project. You can make a bracelet first, then repeat the same steps but larger to make a belt, pet collar, or other projects.

Materials

3 pieces of yarn, each about 8 inches long

Needle and thread

Button with a shank (a loop on the back for sewing in place, instead of holes through the center)

❀ Knot the three pieces of yarn together at one end. Slip the knot into a drawer and gently close it—this will hold the end for you as you braid.

Braid following this pattern

1 2 3   2 3 1   3 2 1   3 1 2

Braid the strands, overlapping them according to the following pat-tern: bring the right strand toward the center and over the middle strand. Take the left strand and cross it over the middle strand. Repeat this pattern with the right strand and then the left, in an alternating fashion until the entire piece is braided. Stitch the ends together with a needle and thread. Sew on a button to one end, using a loop on the other end as a buttonhole to clasp your bracelet.

Make a Wheat Dolly

Centuries ago, farmers in Europe made a decorative wreath called a wheat dolly after the harvest, then planted it in the ground along with seeds in the spring. They hoped it would bring them good luck and a better crop. You can hang yours on the wall, put it on a Christmas tree, or give it to a friend. Make several, and hope they bring you good luck!

Materials

Wheat straws with the heads on
Hot water
Pan
Sewing thread
Scissors
Towel (optional)
Heavy object (such as a large book)

♣ Soak the wheat straws in a pan of hot water for half an hour or so. That will make them flexible and pliable. They will be easier to bend without breaking.

Lay three pieces of straw together; then tie them with a piece of thread just below the heads. Knot securely and clip the thread.

Straw hats are now mostly machine-made, but handmade hats have been popular throughout history. Straw hats are made by splitting the straw into lengthwise pieces, or splits. A single piece of straw can be divided into three to seven splits, depending upon how delicate and fine the braid will be. In Switzerland, delicately woven bands that looked like lace were made from very thinly split straw. Rolls of the straw lace were sold around the world to ladies' hat-makers, called milliners. Hundreds of thousands of people made a living making straw hats at home or in factories. If you look closely at a straw hat today, you can see how rounds of twisted straw are machine-stitched together to create the hat. Other styles may be woven by machine, then pressed into shape over a form.

You may want to work on a towel to keep the straws from sliding around. Lay a heavy object, like a book, on the straw heads to hold the piece in place to make braiding easier.

Braid the three stems, keeping the strands flat on the table. Bend each piece at the sides as you braid so it stays flat. The wet straw will bend but not break. Rewet the straws now and then if they become dry.

Keep braiding until the piece is 8 or more inches long. When a straw is too short to continue, cut the head off a fresh piece and slip it over the top of the other to continue. When it's as long as you want, tie the end together with thread and trim the ends evenly. Bring the bottom of the braid up to the back of the heads of wheat. Tie it in place with thread.

You can tie a bow or glue beads, feathers, or trim to cover the thread. It's ready to hang on the wall or use as a holiday tree ornament.

In Japan, a yearly Straw Festival celebrates the rice harvest. Artists create larger-than-life sculptures from rice straw. See http://en.rocketnews24.com/2013/10/19/the-giant-straw-sculptures-of-japan/.

The American Museum of Straw Art in Long Beach, California, has an educational website with lots of information about straw artistry. Their website is www.strawartmuseum.org.

Braid and Felt Shoelaces

*E*veryone needs shoelaces. Why not make some that look different from the average ones and use some of your extra yarn, too?

This project uses two skills: braiding and felting. Both are skills people learned thousands of years ago. No equipment is required, either.

To start, you need to be sure you use wool yarn. Remember, it is the fiber that will felt together. Plant yarns, like cotton and linen; plastic yarns, like acrylic; and machine-washable superwash wool yarn won't felt. And you won't need too much yarn, so using up some leftovers will work great—as long as the yarn is wool.

Materials

8 to 10 yards of bulky wool yarn, in 3 different colors. That's a total of 24 to 30 yards of yarn. You can make the laces all one color, but 3 make it really artistic.

Measuring tape

Scissors

3 rubber bands

Hot water

Bar of soap or liquid dishwashing soap

Cold water

Vinyl tape such as electrical tape. Use a color to match the laces, or black.

♣ Decide how long you want the laces to be, depending upon how many pairs of eyelets the shoes have. Then double that number. That's because the braiding and felting will shrink the length. Look at the chart below. Laces that will fit a shoe with five pairs of eyelets are about 39 inches, so you'll need 78 inches of yarn (2 x 39 = 78). Then, because you want to make a *pair* of laces, you'll need to cut enough to make two matching laces. Since you will be using three pieces of yarn for each lace, you'll need six pieces of yarn, each the same length.

4 pairs of eyelets: 35" finished lace (cut 70" pieces)

5 pairs of eyelets: 39" finished lace (cut 78" pieces)

6 pairs of eyelets: 43" finished lace (cut 86" pieces)

7 pairs of eyelets: 47" finished lace (cut 94" pieces)

8 pairs of eyelets: 51" finished lace (cut 102" pieces)

Once you've got the six pieces of yarn cut, separate them into two groups, with three different colors in each group. Knot one end to hold them together.

Separate the three strands and roll each one into a ball, up to half the length of the yarn. Wrap a rubber band around the ball to hold it together. As you braid, keep unrolling and rerolling the yarn as you need it. This will keep it from becoming a tangled mess as you braid.

Slip the knot into a drawer, then close the drawer and it will hold the braid securely as you work. No drawer around? Hold the knotted end between your knees, pressing

Tuck the ends in a drawer to hold

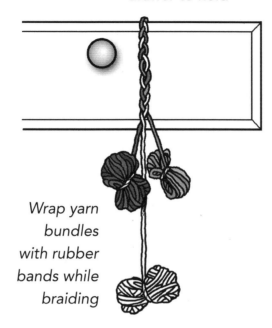

Wrap yarn bundles with rubber bands while braiding

your knees tight to hold it as you braid.

Braid the three pieces together, wrapping one side yarn over the center yarn, then the other side yarn over the center yarn. Side-over-center, side-over-center . . . Keep up the pattern. Don't braid too tightly; the felting process will make the braid tighter. When you

reach the end of the strands and the braid is complete, knot the ends together to keep the braid from coming apart.

Now begin felting. Using hot tap water, dip the braid in the sink to wet it completely. The hot water makes the scales on the sides of wool fiber open up. Then they can get tangled together to make felt. Rub the wet lace on a bar of soap to make suds, then keep rubbing the lace and rolling it between your hands. Check to be sure the laces don't felt to themselves. Open the lace up now and then, and roll it lengthwise between your palms. Dip it in hot water again and continue sudsing and rubbing. The soap makes the scales slide together easier.

Once the braid has become felt, it will be solid and the pieces of yarn won't separate at all. Then rinse it in hot water again, followed by a rinse in cold water. That will smooth any fuzzy edges of yarn into place. Squeeze the water out, and hang to dry. Repeat the whole process of braiding and felting to make your second lace.

Once the laces are dry, you need to put aglets on. *Aglets* are the solid pieces at the end of laces that help them thread through eyelets and keep the laces from unraveling. With scissors, trim the knotted ends off the laces. Cut a piece of colorful tape (or use black if you want) and wrap it tightly around the end. You've made an aglet! Make three more, on the ends of both laces.

You can use strips of felted laces to make other things, like pet leashes, lanyards, bracelets, pony-tail wraps, or other ideas. It's a fun way to use leftover yarn pieces—as long as they are wool.

Wrap tape on the ends to make aglets

Braid a Rug

Braided rugs have been around for a long time. They are useful items that can be made from discarded clothing. Clothing fabric is cut into strips, then braided to make a long rope, which is coiled and stitched into place. A small rug is perfect for a dog or cat to nap on. Make a small mat to use as a hot pad or decoration if you don't have enough time or scraps to make a rug. It's easiest to make a doll-size rug, like this project, first, to get the feel of it, before you take on a larger rug.

Materials

Strips of cloth, about ½-inch wide (an old sheet or T-shirt is perfect for this)
Large safety pin
Needle
Heavy-duty thread
Scissors

❧ You'll need three strips of cloth to begin braiding. Use a large safety pin to hold the ends together. You can slip this end into a drawer to hold it in place for easy braiding.

Following the directions for the braided bracelet on page 12, begin braiding. Lay the left side over center, right side over that one, and so on. When a fabric strip ends, attach another with a few stitches using a threaded needle, and keep going. Continue to braid, adding new strips as needed. When you have a few feet of braid to work with, you can begin sewing it into a rug.

Take out the safety pin and lay the braid on a table. Tightly coil the braid around itself, tucking the ends in and keeping it flat on the table. If it comes unbraided as you coil it, use safety pins to hold it in place, removing them as you work. Use a threaded needle to sew the braid together. Start stitching in the center, and work toward the outside edge as you continue coiling the braid. Take long stitches, but hide them inside the braid as you work, so they don't show very much.

When you get to the end of the braid, tuck the strips inside the coil and stitch over the ends to hide them.

Coil the braid and stitch it together

Knot Tying

For most fiber handcrafts, you'll need to know how to tie a knot or several types of knots. Here are the most commonly used knots.

Square knot: Both ends cross over each other. This is the most basic knot, one you probably already use for everyday things, such as tying your shoes. You can use it to join pieces of yarn together.

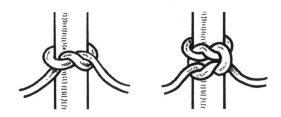

Square knot

Slipknot: Wrap yarn in a loop around two fingers, crossing the yarn coming from the ball over the top of the tail of the yarn. With the other hand, pull the yarn you are working with (the *working yarn*) up through the loop from back to front so it forms a second loop. Hold onto the second loop, slip it over a knitting needle or crochet hook, and pull the tail to tighten and create a knot.

Knot threads for hand sewing: Thread a needle, then pull a tail, leaving the other end long enough that it won't slip through the needle while working. Wrap the long end of the thread tail around your index finger two times.

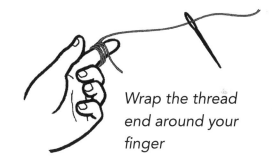

Wrap the thread end around your finger

Roll the loop toward the end of your finger. That rolling will twist the thread loops together.

Roll the loops to the fingertip

Slide the loops off your fingertip and pull the ball of looped thread tight. It should be knotted together firmly. If it is loose, undo it and roll the knot again.

Pull the end and the knot will roll together

If you are sewing with a doubled piece of thread, thread the needle, then pull both ends together, making sure the ends meet evenly. Wrap the ends together in a loop around your index finger and roll toward the fingertip, making a knot of twisted loops.

Needle Hitching

Needle hitching is a pattern of knots. It is an easy way to cover an object, such as a drinking bottle, jar, or anything solid. Cover a jar with needle hitching, then use it as a pencil holder. You could cover a large jar, then center a small candle inside. Cover a water bottle with needle hitching and add a loop to hang it on your bicycle.

Materials

Yarn or thin cord, like kite string
Large-eyed needle (like a crewel needle or yarn needle)
Water bottle, or any plastic drink bottle, with a cap
Scissors

❧ Thread one end of the yarn through the needle. Wrap it around the top of the bottle opening. Tie a square knot (see page 19) to hold it and begin working the "hitch pattern" shown. Work around and around until you cover the sides of the bottle.

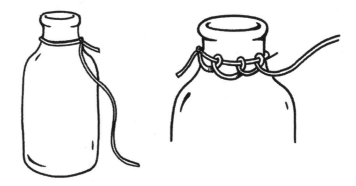

Turn the bottle over and keep going, pulling the knots tight around the base of the bottle. When you get to the end, cut the yarn and tie it in a knot. Tuck the end of the yarn up inside the hitching to hide it.

Cut a length of yarn long enough to make the hanging loop, plus about 6 inches. Tie each end around the top of the bottle to make a secure loop.

Coiled and Stitched Basket

Baskets, mats, and even boats were made by wrapping fibers into a rope, then coiling that rope into rounds and stitching it in place. This project makes a round, flat mat that can be used in many ways.

Materials

Yarn
Yarn needle
Clothesline rope
Scissors

❧ Thread the needle with a doubled length of yarn, knotted at the end. Stitch into the end of the rope, then make another stitch about an inch away. Pull the stitches tight to start the beginning of the coil. Continue coiling the rope around as you wrap yarn over the outside edge of rope and stitch it to the previous round. When the mat is as large as you want, cut the rope end, then wrap several stitches over the cut end to hide it.

You can make a coiled basket by wrapping the base just like the directions above, then slipping the rope on top of the previous round for the next round of stitching. Build the sides up from that round, until the basket is as tall as you like, then cut the rope and tuck the cut end under a few yarn stitches to hide it. People have coiled grass, willow branches—even pine needles—to make baskets.

ROUND AND ROUND
Spinning

We spin fibers to make yarn. Why? If you try using plain fibers, they fall apart from each other and are pretty much only useful as stuffing. If you want to use fiber to make cord or yarn, twisting is a must.

In the Stone Age, people twisted fibers together with their hands, rolling the fiber against their thighs. As the twisted cord got longer, they rolled it into a ball, until someone realized that rolling onto a stick worked better. From there, it wasn't long until others figured out that using a stick to help twist the fibers into a roll was even faster. Adding something to the bottom of the stick made it roll easier, and you could hold it in the air to spin around faster, so the fibers would roll together more easily. Soon, the hand (or drop) spindle was invented. The oldest spindles

we have found are about 7,000 years old, but people have been spinning with spindles for 20,000 years. It wasn't until the 13th century that spinning wheels were invented.

The first spindles were made of sticks, with a weight (called a whorl) that could be many things: clay, beeswax, a sea shell, or a rock. After spinning wheels became common, people still used hand spindles because they could be carried everywhere. Any spare time could be used to make yarn, without toting a heavy wheel along. When you had to spin all the yarn needed to make the family's clothing, you didn't want to waste time.

As you will discover, hand spinning is fun. It's relaxing to do and very satisfying to make a lovely yarn.

Spin by Hand

Before anyone invented a spindle, people spun yarn and cord with just their hands. Give it a try; you don't need to buy any special tools to get started.

Materials

3 or more cotton balls or cotton from pill bottles

❧ Take a small bunch of cotton fibers and pull them apart a little so they're long and loose. Roll one end between your palms or down your thigh with the flat of your hand while holding onto the other end. Do it over and over, stopping to gently pull the ends of the cotton to stretch it into a yarn shape. It will get longer and longer. The fibers will wrap around each other as they twist during the rolling—or spinning—process.

Stretch out another cotton ball and pull gently on the end to blend it into the twisted fiber you've been spinning. Continue working, adding more cotton as you go. You can use a small stick, like a pencil, to wrap the end of the curling yarn around so it won't become twisted.

It will get more difficult to handle, with the yarn curling up unless it's wrapped on a stick. That's how people learned to create spindles to wrap the yarn around.

Pull a cotton ball apart

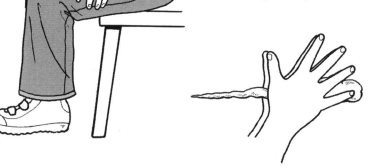

To spin, roll the cotton with the palms of your hands or on your thigh

Make a Hand (Drop) Spindle

The spinning wheel wasn't invented until the 13th century, about 800 years ago. Before that everyone relied on what we call drop spindles. A drop spindle hangs in the air; it's "dropped" to spin and twist fibers into yarn, rather than rolling the fibers on one's thigh. It's lots of fun to spin with a drop spindle. It's clean, quiet, and very portable. It uses no electricity, so you can enjoy spinning yarn just about anywhere.

Materials

¼-inch-thick wooden dowel, about 12 inches long
3 rubber bands
Wooden wheel, 2 inches to 3 inches in diameter (sold in craft stores)
2 metal fender washers (optional, sold in hardware stores)
24 inches of yarn

♣ Wrap a rubber band around the dowel 3 inches from one end. Slide the wheel onto the dowel from the other end, pressing it against the rubber band. Wrap a rubber band around the dowel, above the wheel, and slide it down to hold the wheel securely in place. It's easiest to wrap the band around the dowel near the end, then roll it down into place against the wheel.

Wrap a rubber band tightly around the other end of the dowel away from the wheel, about 1 inch from that end of the dowel. It will give you something to grip with your fingers as you spin the dowel, and will help keep the yarn from slipping off the shaft.

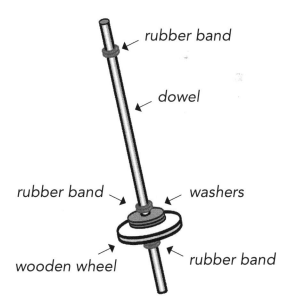

rubber band

dowel

rubber band

washers

wooden wheel

rubber band

Now you have a spindle, with a *shaft* (the dowel part) and a *whorl* (the wheel part). As you learn to spin, you may find it easier to spin if you add more weight to the spindle. You can go back and slip a metal washer (or two) onto the shaft, just above the wheel, rolling the rubber bands back into place to hold everything. The washers will add just enough weight to make spinning easier.

Before you can spin, you need to add a piece of yarn to the spindle, which is called a leader—it will help lead the fibers into place. As the leader spins and twists, it will pick up fibers and twist them, too, and your yarn will grow from the leader. A leader can be any color, because you will cut your yarn off from it when you are finished.

Make a slipknot on one end of the leader and slide it down around the shaft, to the whorl. Bring the yarn down under

the whorl and wrap it around the shaft below the whorl two or three times; then bring the yarn back up and make a half-hitch loop to hold the leader onto the shaft. Be sure the loop goes under the leader, and the spindle will hang steady when you hold the end of the leader. There should be about 12 inches of loose leader above the half-hitch.

Holding the spindle by the end of the leader, give it a twirl clockwise and watch it spin. As it spins, the leader will twist. That twist is the secret of spinning. The twisting leader will pick up other fibers as it continues twisting, and the wrapping will create yarn that will hold together.

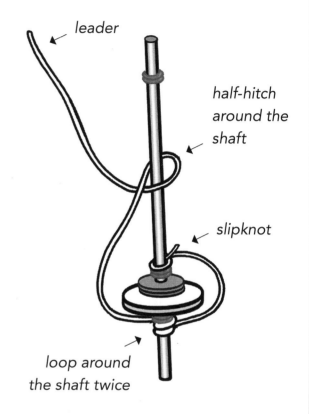

leader

half-hitch around the shaft

slipknot

loop around the shaft twice

Slipknot

Ply Yarn on a Hand Spindle

If you pull apart a strand of yarn, you'll see that it's made of several tinier strands of yarn that are twisted together. Each strand is called a ply, and when two or more thin pieces are twisted together, they are plied. Yarns are sold as two-ply, three-ply, or more.

Materials

Spindle
Two balls of yarn, different colors
2 large bowls or shoe boxes

❦ You can do this activity easily, even if you haven't spun before. These directions are written for right-handed people. If you are left-handed, just switch when you come to points directing the use of one hand or the other.

Start plying with the two different colors of yarn, rolled in separate balls. Put the two balls in bowls or shoe boxes to keep them from rolling around the floor as you work with them. Stand up, holding the ends of both yarns in your left hand, letting the ends dangle about 6 inches. Holding the end of the leader with your left hand, set the spindle spinning with your right hand. Once it's spinning, move the leader to your right finger and thumb.

Lay the yarn ends you'll be plying over the top of your left hand, and dangling onto the spinning leader. As it twists tighter, it will begin picking up the yarns, and pulling them into the twist.

Spinning happens here where the twist begins

Once they are caught up in the twist of the leader, let the yarn drop downward a bit and new yarn will pull into the twist. Let go of the leader and let it spin the twist. Keep going—you're spinning!

When plying, you want to spin the yarns in the *opposite* direction, so they will cling around each other as they twist. That means you must twirl the spindle *counterclockwise* when spinning to ply. Using the techniques in the Drop Spindle project (see page 25), spin both yarns together, wrapping them on the spindle as you go.

Yarns from two balls

The ends catch in the spinning twist of the leader yarn

When the spindle reaches the floor, it's time to unwind the yarn and roll it onto the spindle. Hold the spindle between your knees, to keep it from unwinding. Keep your left thumb and finger pinched on the end of the twist, so it won't keep pulling the yarns together. Pull the yarn loop up and off the spindle; then carefully roll the yarn you just plied onto the shaft of the spindle. Wind it tight and smoothly, starting near the whorl and working upward and outward. Leave enough to wrap twice under the whorl and to make another hitch on the shaft, and continue like you did before.

The yarn you create will be very twisty when you take it off the spindle, so let it relax just a bit,

and the twists will ease. That's it! You have created a unique yarn. Roll the new yarn into a ball to use on a project later.

You can also ply your own hand-spun yarn. When you have spun enough yarn to make two balls of yarn, put them in boxes or bowls and try making a two-ply yarn using your own hand-spun singles. Just ply them together onto the spindle, but with a big difference—remember, you'll be plying in a *counterclockwise* direction with the spindle.

Spin Fiber on a Spindle

Ready to spin fiber? It's easiest to spin wool at first, and as you gain more skill you can move on to silk, cotton, linen, alpaca, mohair, cashmere—the world of fiber awaits! But it's best to learn to spin with wool, because it has just enough crimp and elasticity to hold itself together into a yarn more easily than other fibers. As you gain more experience, the other fibers will be easy, too.

Materials

Wool that has been washed, then combed or carded, sometimes called roving

Spindle

❖ Use wool that has been washed, then combed or carded. That will make it easier to spin because the hairs are already lined up.

Pull off a strip of the fiber, about 1 inch thick. Start at one end, holding the strip between both hands with thumb and forefinger, about 3 inches apart. Gently pull the fiber apart a bit, not enough that it breaks, but enough to stretch and line up the hairs even more. It should be about as thick as a thick crayon or marker.

Continue working along the rest of the strip, pulling gently to lengthen the strip. Roll it up, wrapping it around your left wrist to keep it out of the way as you spin. Then you can feed the end of it into the twist as you work.

You'll spin fiber just like you did when you plied yarns together in the previous activity. Following those directions, begin spinning fiber by draping the end down over your left hand, letting a few inches hang freely so it gets caught in the spin of the leader.

Then, holding the leader in your left hand briefly, give the spindle a twirl with your right hand. Spin it clockwise by pinching your right thumb and fingers around the rubber band at the top of the shaft. Once it gets going, let the fiber twist into the leader yarn while the spindle spins on its own.

Give the spindle a twirl whenever it stops spinning.

Be sure that you don't ever let the twist run up the un-spun fiber. Keep your finger and thumb tightly pinched on the yarn you are spinning so the twist doesn't run up the fiber uncontrolled.

Mohandas Gandhi led an independence movement in India in the early 20th century. India had a thriving cotton and cloth industry, which the British government took over as a colonial power. Britain wanted cotton for the new mechanical looms in England as the Industrial Age began. They forced India to ship cotton to England, and then the Indian people had to purchase English-made cloth for their own clothing.

As the Indian people united to force the British out of their country, they boycotted English cloth. They refused to buy it. They began wearing hand-spun, handwoven cloth. Spinning became patriotic in India. Gandhi appeared in public wearing only simple clothing made of hand-spun cloth as a political act. He used a small portable spinning wheel as a symbol of independence from Britain. Finally, Britain gave India its independence. Today India exports fiber and fabric to many countries.

When you stop spinning to adjust the yarn on the spindle, keep that pinch in place to keep the twist under control.

Once you have spun enough new yarn that the spindle is almost to the floor, it's time to stop and wind the yarn onto the spindle. Keeping the twist pinched with your left hand, hold the spindle between your knees to keep it from moving. Slip the loop off the shaft and unwind the yarn below the whorl. Keeping it taut so it doesn't unwind, roll it up onto the spindle, above the whorl. Leave enough to wrap twice around the shaft beneath the whorl, then loop onto the shaft, and a few inches for the new leader. Pull the last loop onto the shaft tightly. You should be able to hold the spindle steady by the end of the leader, ready to give it another spin to get going.

From here, continue just as you did, feeding stretched lengths of fiber onto the twist. Wrap new yarn around the spindle until it won't hold any more; then wind it off into a ball for use later.

You'll find that as you gain experience with spinning, the yarn will spin finer and thinner. Save the yarn you make at first, so you can compare later and see your progress. With practice, everyone begins to make thinner and thinner yarn. Many spinners say that over time they cannot easily make the thick yarn they had spun in the beginning.

James Hargreaves, an Englishman, invented the spinning machine in the late 1700s. He wanted to save work for his wife and daughters. Jealous neighbors destroyed his first machine and ran him out of town because they thought the machine was unfair competition. His invention helped Britain become the world leader in textile production.

Winding Yarn

Some yarn is sold in loosely coiled or wound skeins (pronounced "skayns") that must be rolled into a ball before you use them. If you don't rewind the yarn into a ball before you start working with it, you'll have a tangled mess. Just remember to keep everything loose and relaxed.

❧ There are three ways to rewind yarn:

+ Have a friend put the skein around their hands to keep it from tangling as you wind the new ball.

+ Use the back of a chair to hold the skein as you stand behind the chair and wind the ball.

+ Use a ball winder that is sold in yarn stores. It works with a hand crank. Sometimes yarn shops will wind the yarn into a ball for you after you buy it—just ask them!

Some yarn is sold in skeins and must be rolled into a ball before using it

A friend can help you wind yarn

Use a chair to help wind yarn

Yarn ball winder— turn the crank and it winds the yarn into a ball

Roll a ball that unwinds from the center. It won't roll around while you work.

Tie a slipknot around an empty tissue tube. Wrap yarn sideways at an angle while turning the tube the opposite direction. Continue wrapping and turning until the yarn makes a ball thick enough to hold together; then slide the ball off the tube, push the slipknot to the center, and continue rolling the ball. When you're finished, the end with the slipknot can be used as your working yarn for a project.

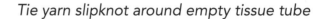

Tie yarn slipknot around empty tissue tube

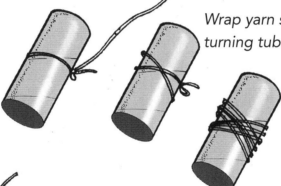

Wrap yarn sideways at an angle while turning tube the opposite direction

Keep wrapping and turning

Pull the yarn off the tube when the ball is thick enough to hold together. Push the slipknot to the center.

Keep rolling the ball at an angle as you add yarn. Reach into the middle to pull the slipknot end out. It will be your working end of yarn.

OVER AND UNDER
Weaving

People began weaving thousands of years ago, using twigs as a loom. Today's looms are more complicated, and large ones are even computer-driven. But all weaving uses the same basic action: lengthwise and crosswise threads are passed over and under each other so that they lock to create fabric. The lengthwise threads (called warp) are tied to a frame (the loom), and the crosswise threads (weft) are passed over and under them. Weaving can be very simple or very complex and can be done with very fine threads to make silk shirts or thick yarns to make rugs. You can tell if a fabric is woven by looking at the tiny thread pattern to see how they pass over and under each other. In knitted fabric—like T-shirts—thread wraps around itself in loops, unlike woven fabric.

A lot of folk tales and stories are about spinners and weavers. In ancient Greece, a story was told of a girl named Arachne who boasted that she could weave better than Athena, the goddess of weaving. After Athena won the weaving contest she turned the girl into a spider to weave webs forever. The Greek word for spider is *arachne*, from which we get our scientific name for spiders, *arachnids*.

String Art Coaster

A simple way to start practicing weaving is by doing a few string art projects that show how it looks when yarn strands are crossed over one another. It's easy to start working with a paper plate, and paper bowls are actually even easier. Because the bowl curves, you have room for your hands to work the weaving process with less tension. This project weaves a small circle, perfect for a drink coaster.

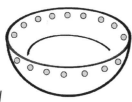

Punch holes in the rim of the paper bowl

Make the holes across from each other. Add one extra hole so there is an odd number of holes.

Materials

Paper bowl (a paper plate will work, too, but a bowl is easier for beginners)

Pencil

Ruler

Hole punch

Yarn

Yarn needle

Scissors

Felt

Glue or needle and thread

♣ With the pencil and ruler, mark points around the bowl's edge that are directly across from each other. Continue until there is a mark about every inch. Add one extra mark, because weaving requires an uneven number of warp threads.

Punch holes at the marked points, all around the bowl. Tie one end of a length of yarn on at one of the holes. Thread the other end with the needle and push yarn through the hole directly across from it.

Tie on the yarn and stitch it into the hole directly across from it. Bring the yarn back out through the hole next to that one. Continue until all the holes are threaded.

Move the needle to the hole next to the one you came down through, and thread the yarn up through it. Then stitch across.

Continue, stitching across, then into the next hole, then across. When all the holes are stitched with yarn, tie the end in a knot, through the last hole. You have now created your *warp* yarn on your paper-bowl loom.

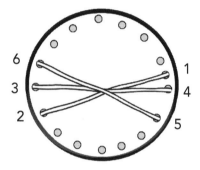

Thread the needle with yarn for the *weft* yarn, which can be a different color if you want. Begin at the center, where the yarns cross each other. Tie the end at the center and begin working around and around, going over then under each warp yarn as you go around the circle. Continue, round after round, adding new yarn as needed and tying it on with a knot. When you are about an inch from the edge, stop and knot the yarn to a warp yarn to secure it. Clip the ends about an inch or more long.

Remove the weaving from the bowl by clipping through the loops that run through the holes along the outer edge. Clip one at a time and knot the two ends together. You'll have an extra end to knot into its neighboring yarn.

To mount the weaving so you can use it for a drink coaster or mouse pad, cut a piece of felt the same size as the woven circle you made. Fold the cut ends of the warp threads to the back to hide them, and stitch or glue the weaving to the piece of felt.

Begin weaving at the center. Go over and under, round and round. Stop about 1 inch from the holes. Clip yarn loops and knot together.

Remove the woven circle from the bowl

Names and Letters

Use *string art to make a large sign with your name on it, or even just a large initial letter. Words like* HOME, JOY, LOVE, PEACE, *or* HAPPY *make nice accents in a room and great gifts for anyone.*

Materials

Foam board, cork board, or small piece of plywood

Paint (optional)

Pencil or chalk

Ruler

Hammer (if using a wood base)

Box of 1-inch-long wire nails, with heads

Kite string, yarn, or crochet thread

❧ If using plywood, paint it and let it dry. Use a pencil or chalk and a ruler to draw the letters you want to use. Use a plain solid letter style for your first project—you can get fancier with the next one.

Hammer or push the nails into position all around the outer edge of the letters and along any inside edges. Keep the nails about ¼ inch apart.

Knot the thread on the first nail in the top left corner. Working with a small ball of yarn, begin winding the yarn around the outline made

by the nails, wrapping it around and pulling tight to keep the yarn taut as you work. You'll be winding counterclockwise (left to right) around nails that are across from each other. After you wind around one nail, do the one directly across from it next. You may have to criss-cross the yarn here and there, to reach all the nails. You want to fill in the center of the letter with yarn strands. Continue all around the letters, going over some nails twice if necessary. When complete, knot the string end. You can do the entire word in the same string, or use different colors for different letters.

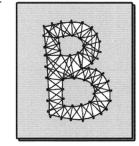

Branch Weaving

Here's a way to weave an over-and-under pattern. You don't need to make a loom—you can use a tree branch, like the very first weavers did.

Materials

Tree or shrub branch with a V shape

Yarn in several colors

Scissors

Yarn needle

Beads, feathers, sea shells, or buttons (optional)

❦ Wrap yarn onto the branch to create the warp. Start at the base of the V, wrapping the yarn around the branch twice to secure it; then stretch across to the other branch, wrap it twice, and continue. Keep the yarn tight. When you get to the end of the branch, knot the yarn and clip the end.

With new yarn, you'll weave the weft onto the warp. Thread the yarn needle with yarn and begin weaving it through the weft yarns. Starting at the V, go over one weft yarn, then under the next. When you get to the end, turn and go back, continuing the over-under pattern. Keep weaving row by row, pushing the weft yarns together with your fingers, to fill in the spaces.

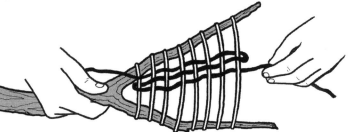

Wrap yarn around the branch for the warp. Then weave yarn over and under.

Change colors of yarn as you weave, and add beads, feathers, sea shells, or buttons if you wish.

When you've woven as much as the branch will hold, knot the weft yarn to a warp strand or the branch, and clip the end. You can hang your woven art on the wall—the branch will be the frame.

Fork Flowers

These little flowers are so fun to make, and they use the tiniest loom: a dinner fork.

Materials

Yarn: any color, plus a piece of green about 8 inches long
Dinner fork with 4 tines
Scissors

❧ These blossoms are tiny, about 1 inch across. Once you've finished one, you will want to make lots more. String them together to make a bracelet or stitch onto a head-band. There are many ways to use these cute little flowers.

Cut a length of green yarn about 8 inches long. Lay it between the two center tines of the fork, with half hanging down each side of the fork. You'll use this piece to tie the flower together.

Hold the end of the blossom yarn in place with one hand and begin wrapping the yarn over and under the fork tines, weaving the yarn around the fork. Turn at the edges and come back, going over and under the opposite tines. It should look like a basket weave pattern. Keep winding until the fork tines are almost covered. Stop winding and cut the end of the yarn, holding the end so that the yarn doesn't slide off the tines.

Pull the two hanging stem yarn ends up over the woven section to pull the woven strings together, tying a tight knot as you pull the blossom off the fork. Fluff the blossom so the petals are all about the same length.

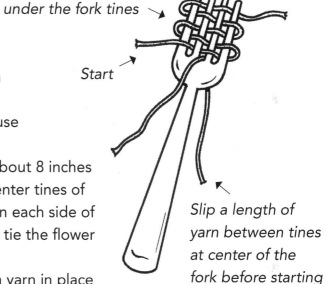

Wrap yarn over and under the fork tines

Start

Slip a length of yarn between tines at center of the fork before starting

Weaving Sticks

People wove using weaving sticks long before they created looms. Children had the job of weaving simple bands of cloth that the family used for tying clothing together. There were no zippers or buttons to hold things, so woven bands were important. You can weave a band to use as a belt, hair band, pet collar, or display on the wall. Weaving sticks are also easy to take along on trips or store in your backpack to use when you get bored.

Materials

5 plastic drinking straws
Hole punch
Scissors
Yarn in several colors

♣ Punch a hole in each straw about ½ inch from one end. It's easier if you flatten the straw as you push it into the hole punch.

Cut the other end of the straws off so the straws are about 6 inches long. That's all you need to create the loom, so now you're ready to tie on the warp.

Cut five lengths of yarn, each 36 inches long. Thread the yarn through the hole in the straw. When all five are threaded with yarns, hold the straws together and pull all the yarn straight so the lengths are even.

Tie the yarn ends together in one loose knot. That will keep your weaving from sliding off the ends of the warp yarn as you work.

Start weaving the weft yarn between the straws. Hold the

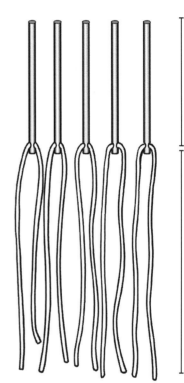

6 inches

Yarn hangs down 18 inches

straws loosely together next to each other in one hand and weave the yarn over one, then under the next, then over, and under. When you get to the last straw in the row, just wrap the yarn around the straw and begin another row going the other direction.

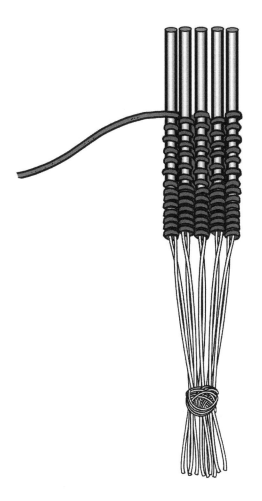

When the weaving is large enough that you reach near the top of the straws, gently push it down onto the hanging warp yarns. Wiggle the straws a bit and it will slide off easier. Don't push the woven section completely off the straws until you are finished. If it slides off, though, just keep on weaving and push it all together later.

Keep weaving until there are about 2 inches of warp yarn left below the bottom edge of the straws. Cut each yarn and tie a knot with the yarn next to it. Untie the bottom knot and tie those yarns together so the woven section won't slide off the bottom warp. Trim the yarn ends, or leave them as fringe.

Weave a Square

For this project, you will make a simple loom from a piece of cardboard. You'll be weaving the same way it has been done for thousands of years. You'll warp the loom, then weave the weft threads into it by passing them over and under the warp.

Materials

Corrugated cardboard, 12 inches square

Pencil

Ruler

Scissors

Yarn, about 10 yards, any colors (roll it in a ball so it's easier to work with)

♣ Measure and mark slits about ½ inch apart along two opposite edges of the cardboard. Count the slits on each side and make certain you end up with an *uneven* number of slits. (This uneven number will make an even number of tabs.) Cut the slits about ½ inch deep.

Thread the warp by pushing the end of the yarn firmly into the first top left slit.

Wrap the yarn around and feed it through the opposite slit on the other edge of the cardboard.

Wrap it around the tab and forward through the next slit. Continue wrapping across the board and around each tab until you've used all the slits. Wind around the last tab twice and knot to secure it if needed. Cut the yarn from the ball of yarn.

Now make the weft—the crosswise threads that are woven between the warp threads. Cut

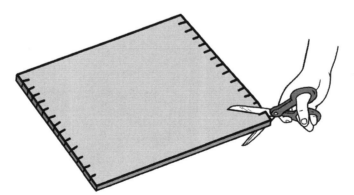

Wrap the warp yarn back and forth around the slits

several pieces of yarn 16 inches long. Start at the top of the loom and weave the yarn over the first warp yarn, under the second, over the third, and then under. Keep making the over-then-under pattern.

reverse the pattern. Start the next weft piece going under, then over. Keep adding more weft pieces, weaving them opposite to the previous row. Change the pattern from over-under to under-over, so every other strand is woven in each row.

Keep going until the whole loom is covered. Then carefully tie each pair of yarn ends at the sides in knots. Bend the loom, so the weaving can be popped off the tabs. Pull the woven piece off the cardboard loom. Pat yourself on the back—you are a weaver!

Weave the weft yarns in and out to make a pattern

When you get to the other end of the loom, adjust the yarn—it should lie flat and even. Now

The Vikings traveled the Atlantic Ocean, even to North America, in wooden ships powered by the wind. The sails on their ships were woven from wool. Viking voyages along the coast of Europe and up the rivers into central Asia were possible because women and children stayed home, spinning and weaving the wool from *lots* of sheep.

A Viking ship's sail took a year's wool from 2,000 sheep. It was spun with drop spindles, then woven into strips of cloth on large upright looms. It took years to make a new sail. Danish king Canute had 1,700 ships at his command when he invaded England in 1085. That took a lot of wool!

Surprisingly, woolen sails make a boat move about 10 percent faster than modern sails, which are made of nylon or polyester.

Weave a Tapestry

*T*apestry weaving is used to make an image or special design. In the Middle Ages, tapestries hung on castle walls to make the cold stone rooms pretty and warm. Native Americans wove tapestry-style blankets. Make a tapestry-style weaving to hang on your own wall, using different colored yarns to make stripes or simple designs like triangles or hearts. In a tapestry, the weft yarn (the one you weave into the warped backing) makes the design. For this project, a baking rack is the warp, so you only add weft yarns.

Materials

Metal baking rack (used to cool cookies. Racks can be purchased in dollar stores and thrift shops in various sizes. For larger projects, use discarded racks from refrigerator shelving.)
Yarns in several colors
Scissors
Large yarn needle (You can do this project without a needle, using only your fingers, but a yarn needle makes it much easier.)

❧ The metal rack acts as both the loom and the warp. All you have to do is start weaving in the weft yarn. Thread the yarn needle with a doubled strand of yarn and knot the ends together. Slip the yarn

around the lower corner of the baking rack, then pass the needle through the knotted end loop. This creates a half-hitch.

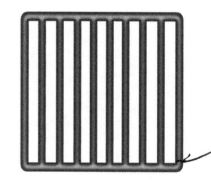

Fasten yarn to the bottom of the rack loom

Then begin the over-and-under pattern of weaving the yarn through the baking rack. When you get to the other edge of the rack, pull the yarn smooth and tight, then wrap the yarn around the end wire twice. Now go back for a second row. This time be sure to alternate, going over the wires you went under for the previous row, then under the wires you went over. When you get to the edge, wrap the yarn twice around the end wire and continue weaving the next row.

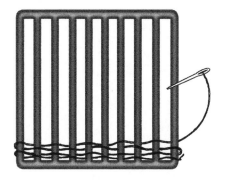

Weave over then under. Alternate to make a basket weave pattern.

Create patterns, stripes, or designs as you weave

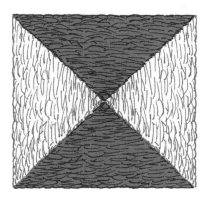

When you run out of yarn, rethread the needle with more, tying the ends together. Keep the knotted ends on the back side of the weaving, so they will be hidden from view.

Once you know how to weave, you can begin planning designs. To make stripes, just change yarn colors when you reach the sides of the loom. To create other designs, you might want to first make a drawing to plan your work. To change yarn colors for the design, bring in the new yarn from the back of the weaving, weaving it in places as you wish, then letting the loose end dangle at the

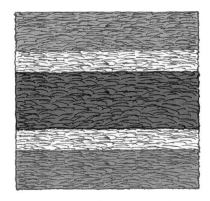

back. Bring the end back through and weave with it when you want that color again. Just be careful to keep the yarns loose at the back so the weaving doesn't pull out of shape as you work.

Push the woven section together from time to time, so the yarn covers most of the wire. When you are finished, knot and clip the yarn ends. Tuck all knots and ends to the back side. Tie and knot any loose ends at the back.

To display your weaving, just hang it from a nail on the wall. The wire rack acts as a loom and a frame. It also makes a good mat for hot pans in the kitchen.

Hula Hoop Rug

This project results in a large finished piece, but it can be done quickly and creates a really neat project that you can use as a rug or hang on the wall.

Materials

One adult-size T-shirt
Scissors
Plastic hula hoop
Fiber for weaving: thick yarns, cord made by finger knitting (see page 50), or 1-inch-wide strips cut from old bedsheets, tablecloths, or clothing

♣ Lay the T-shirt flat and trim away the sleeves, neck, and bottom hem. Cut across the shirt, cutting through front and back at the same time, making strips 1 to 2 inches wide. Make 16 strips.

Lay the hula hoop flat and work with two loops of T-shirt strips at once. Stretch eight pairs of T-shirt loops across the hoop, moving around the hoop as you go until it looks like a bicycle wheel. The T-shirt strips will be the *warp* for the loom.

Use this section

Cut into 16 strips, from side to side

Stretch eight pairs of loops across the hoop for the warp

For the *weft*, the yarn you weave onto the loom, roll strips of fabric or yarn about 2 to 3 yards long into small bundles. Begin at the center of the warp, wrapping the weft strips over and under each pair of warp strips. Weave the warp strips as pairs, meaning weave over and under the front and back of two of them at once.

Continue the over-under weaving, around and around, until you've woven a center circle that's about 8 inches across.

Now the big change: from that point, begin weaving over and under each warp loop one at a time, separately. Remember that each warp loop has two parts, the front and back.

Continue weaving, adding more yarn as you need it by tying a knot and rolling up a new bundle to weave with.

Keep weaving over and under the warp strips until you are about 4 inches from the rim of the hoop. Cut the warp strips off the hoop and tie them together in twos using square knots. That will keep the rug from coming apart. Tuck the ends inside the weaving to hide them, or leave them as a fringe. Ta-daa! Your rug is finished.

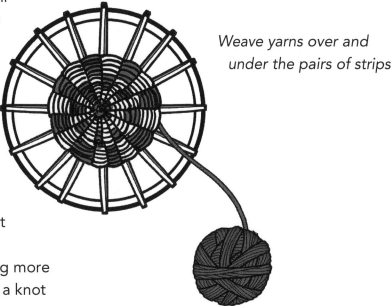

Weave yarns over and under the pairs of strips

Weave a Cup Basket

Weaving can be done on a flat surface, using a loom, but it can also be done in three dimensions. Baskets are woven without looms and can be just as easy to get started. This little basket is quick and easy to make. The cup acts as the warp, and all you have to do is weave in the weft yarns. Go over and under, and because you use an uneven number of warp (the strips of cup), the yarn will alternate each time. It's a pattern. Use the little basket to hold pet treats, coins, or snacks. Make one for each of your friends in different yarn colors.

Materials

Paper cup or yogurt cup
Pencil
Scissors
Yarn, one or several colors

❧ Use the pencil to make marks around the top of the cup every ½ inch, or about as far apart as your finger width. Be sure you have an *even* number of marks. You may have to make one or two marks at less than ½ inch to come out with an even number. Using scissors, cut from each mark straight to the base of the cup, making an *uneven* number of strips.

Cut an odd number of strips in the cup. Weave yarn over and under the strips.

Begin weaving yarn between the strips, starting at the bottom of the cup. Hide the loose end under the weaving. Weave over and under each strip in a pattern all the way around. Push the weaving down to hide the cup as you work. When you get to the rim, clip the yarn off and tuck the end back under the weaving.

You can use the same technique to make larger baskets over warps made from ice cream tubs or other lightweight cardboard or plastic containers. Instead of yarn, try weaving strips of fabric cut from old clothes, finger-knitted cord (see page 50), or plarn (plastic + yarn) from recycled plastic bags (see page 135).

IT'S JUST LOOPS
Knitting

Many stockings, sweaters, and caps aren't woven, they are knitted. Knitting is a skill that uses two sticks, called needles (or pins, in some countries). Using the two sticks, loops are pulled through each other, continuing row by row, to create fabric.

When you make a knitted project you are making both the fabric and the parts to the finished project.

It can seem complicated, but it's not. And if you don't like the way a project turns out, just pull the yarn to unravel it and begin again. In fact, unraveling as you go is such a common part of knitting that it has a name: frogging. So, as you knit, relax. It's OK to make mistakes. You can always frog it and start over.

Learn to Finger Knit

To get a feel for knitting (yes, pun intended!), you can knit with only your fingers—no needles necessary.

Knitting without tools, using only one's fingers, started about 3,000 years ago. While it looks like you are weaving, you really are knitting, because the definition of knitting is pulling loops through other loops. The loops are made in rows, and as the loops in each row are pulled through the previous row of loops, a row is dropped off and becomes fabric.

Knitting with two needles was invented about 1,000 years ago, in the Middle East. The purl stitch, another type of stitch used in knitting, emerged in Spain about 500 years ago. The oldest knitted item we know of is a cotton sock remnant found in Egypt.

Today we knit with two sticks, by pulling loops through loops. We work the rows from right to left—opposite to how we read text. That's likely because Arabic, the language of the Middle East, is written and read from right to left.

Materials

Just some yarn and your fingers!

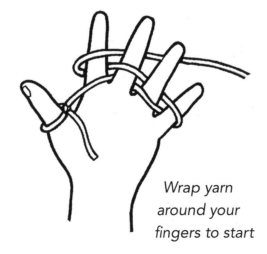

Wrap yarn around your fingers to start

✿ Tie a slipknot (see page 19) and slide the loop onto your thumb. Begin wrapping yarn over and under your four fingers, doing two rows. Then pull the first row's loops up and over the second row, and off your fingers, leaving the second row of loops on your fingers. Wrap another row of yarn over and under the fingers, then pull the lower loops up and over your finger tips. (It helps to bend your fingers to make it easier to pull the loops through.)

Keep wrapping yarn as you pull loops up through the yarn to create a new row of loops

Push the remaining loops back down to the base of your fingers as you continue the process.

The knitted cord of yarn will fall away at the back of your hand. When you're ready to end the work, you'll pull loops over and through each other, which is called binding off. Pull the loop off your index finger and place it on your middle finger. Pull the lower loop on the middle finger up and over the new loop and off your finger. Then pull the remaining loop on your middle finger over and place it on your ring finger. Pull the lower loop up and over the new loop and off your finger, and place the remaining loop on your pinkie finger. Pull the last loop up and over that new loop and off your finger. You'll have one last loop on your pinkie. Clip the end of the yarn and pull the tail through the last loop firmly to make a secure knot.

You can use your cord as a necklace, belt, or bracelet, or make several cord sections and connect them to make projects.

Finger Knit a Scarf

This is a free-form and flex-ible project. You can make as many sections as you like, add a button or just knot the ends together, and add tassels to the ends (see page 67 for how to make a tassel). A thick yarn works best. Dig through your yarn stash and you will likely find several small balls that will be perfect for this project.

Materials

Yarn (amount varies with your design, but thicker yarn works better than thin)
Yarn needle
Large button (optional)

❧ Using the finger knitting technique (page 50), make three knitted sections, each about 48 inches long. Lay the three together and knot them together about 8 inches from each end. If you'd like a thicker scarf, you can knit more sections to tie together.

The ends won't all hang evenly due to varying tension (stretchiness) and stitch size. You can add tassels to some of the ends for an interesting effect.

Thread a yarn needle with matching yarn and sew a large button on top of the knot at one end. Slip the scarf around your neck and fasten by slipping the button through a loop from one of the opposite ends.

Spool Knitting

People knitted with small loom-type frames before they began knitting with two needles. The fabric came out as a long cord. The cords made great fasteners and ties long before zippers and Velcro tape were invented. People sewed the cords together in rounds to make larger items.

Using a simple spool-shaped loom is called knitting Nancy, French knitting, or corking. It's easy and fun to do. You can buy plastic spool-type looms in craft stores, or make your own. Kits come with a hook-shaped tool, like a crochet hook, to lift the loops off the pins.

With this homemade loom, you won't need a tool. The loops can be lifted with your fingers if you don't pull the yarn too tight.

Materials

4 nails, each about 3 inches long
Bathroom tissue tube, or other cardboard tube cut down to about 4 inches in length
Duct tape
Yarn
Scissors

Use 3-inch nails. Position four nails around a cardboard tube. Wrap duct tape around several times to secure the nails and strengthen the tube.

❉ Build the loom by securing four nails to one end of the tube. Position them equally apart from each other on the outside of the tube, with about 1 inch sticking out past the end of the tube. Tape them in place securely with duct tape. Then begin wrapping the entire tube with tape to make it stiff.

Wrap more tape around the nails, pressing it tight to hold them in place. When the tube is solid and sturdy, you're ready to begin.

Work loosely, so you can lift the loops easily. Begin by dropping the end of the working yarn down through the nail end of the tube. Pull the tail through the other end of the tube and hold it against the tube with your thumb while you work the first row, so it won't come undone.

Working yarn

Drop the end of the yarn through the tube. Hold the end in place with your thumb to get started.

Wrap the working yarn clockwise around each nail, moving counterclockwise around the tube until all four nails are looped. You

Wrap yarn around each post (nail) going clockwise. Wrap clockwise around each nail as you move counterclockwise around the tube.

won't wrap loops around the nails from here on. Instead, lay the yarn across the front of the next nail, just above the loop that's on the nail. Then pick up the loop that's on the nail and pull it up and over the new yarn and off the nail. Leave the new yarn on the nail as a new loop. Do the same to the rest of the nails, continuing counterclockwise round after round. The stitches that you pull off and drop into the center become cord, and

Now wrap yarn across the front of the next nail. Pull the loop already on the nail up and over the nail. That leaves a new loop on the nail. Keep working—the knitting will drop down through the center of the tube.

Pull the loop up and over

it will begin to emerge from the bottom of the tube.

Once you get going, you can make miles of lovely cord. You will want to bind off when the cord is as long as you want it, so here's how to do that without unraveling your work.

Take the last loop you made off its nail and put it on the next nail, above the loop on the nail. Pull that loop up and over the new one. Keep moving loops around, until you have only one left. Use scissors to cut the working yarn, leaving a tail about 3 inches long. Pull the end of the yarn tail through the last loop. Pull it up tight to knot it securely.

Use the cord you made for ties, or loop it and stitch to make flowers. To make a headband, slip a plastic headband inside the center of the cord, then stitch or knot the ends securely to keep it in place.

Homemade Knitting Needles

These are fun to make if you are working with a club or group because you can make them ahead of time for everyone to use. They make a nice treat for guests if you are having friends over for a knitting party, too.

Materials

Wooden cooking skewers or chopsticks

Pencil sharpener (for chopsticks)

Fingernail file or scrap of sandpaper

Pony beads, clay, or small pom-poms

Glue

❧ Wooden cooking skewers make about size 6 needles. You can cut them in half, which will make it easier for small hands to control the needles. Glue a bead, clay ball, or small pom-pom to the end, then rub the pointed end lightly with sandpaper or a nail file to smooth any rough spots.

If you want to use chopsticks, sharpen a point on the end with a pencil sharpener, then smooth it with the sandpaper. Glue a bead, clay ball, or pom-pom to the other end. Chopsticks make about size 9 or 10 needles.

Glue beads onto skewers or chopsticks

Want to try knitting without the bother, just to see if it's for you? Why not recycle two plastic automatic pencils? Paper Mate's Sharpwriter yellow plastic pencils are fun to try. A pair of plastic pencil knitting needles are the same as size 11 needles and will hold 20 cast-on stitches. It's fun to do, and one way to get some knitting done if you are stranded on a desert island with only plastic pencils!

Get Started with Needle Knitting

You will need some basic supplies and to learn some basic techniques to begin a knitting project. (Tip: The directions are for right-handed people. If you are left-handed, you'll have to use the opposite term [left instead of right] when you come to it in the directions that follow.)

Supplies

Yarn: A worsted weight is best, and the most common thickness. If you work with wool yarn, remember that the finished project must be washed by hand or it will shrink in the laundry. You may want that if you are felting your project, but be aware.

You may need to first make a ball of your yarn, to make it easy and tangle-free to work with.

Some yarn comes in skeins, which are bundles of looped yarn. It may be wrapped so you can pull an end out and work without tangles. If not, you'll have to wind the yarn into a ball. Look at the Winding Yarn project (page 32) to learn how.

To keep the yarn ball from rolling around while you knit, you can set it in a bowl. Set the bowl on the table or floor as you work. Then as you pull on the working yarn, the ball doesn't roll across the floor.

Knitting Needles: Knitting needles come in a variety of sizes. You can find inexpensive sets at thrift shops or craft and fabric supply stores. You will need two needles of the same size for any project. Some knitting needles are called

circular needles because they help you knit in a tube shape. They are made of two needle ends connected with a piece of plastic cord. You can use them just like a pair of regular needles, too.

The best choice for beginning knitters is a set of size 8 needles with double points (both ends are pointed), called DPNs. They are shorter than regular needles and easier for smaller hands to work with. Wrap one end on each needle with a rubber band to keep the stitches from sliding off the point.

Yarn Needle: A plastic one is easiest to use. A yarn needle has an eye large enough to slide yarn through and doesn't have a sharp point, so it won't snag the yarn. You will need one to sew pieces of a project together.

Scissors

Tape Measure or Ruler: This is important for most projects so you know what size your finished item will be.

Techniques

Make a Slipknot: Use a slipknot every time you tie yarn onto a knitting needle or crochet hook to start a project. To begin, pull a length of yarn from the ball. The end of the yarn that comes from the ball is called the working yarn, and the other end is the tail. Always leave a few inches for a tail, which later you'll slip inside the stitches of your finished project so no cut ends show.

Make a loop and twist it to lay on top of the working yarn to make a yarn "pretzel." Slip the knitting needle (or crochet hook) into the middle of the pretzel and out the other side.

Tie on a slipknot to start

Pull the tail snugly to tighten the knot. The loop should be just loose enough that it can slide on the needle a little.

How to Cast On: Once your slipknot is in place, you'll use it to *cast on* stitches. To cast on, hold the needle with the slipknot in your right hand and loop the working yarn around your left thumb. Then move the needle toward you a little so the yarn crosses itself,

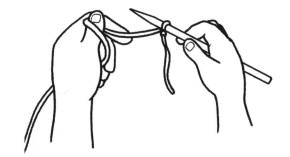

Attach the yarn with a slipknot. Make a loop over your thumb.

closing the loop on your thumb. Insert the needle in the loop from below and slip the loop off your thumb and onto the end of the needle. Pull snug, but not tight. Each loop on the needle is called a stitch.

Slip the yarn loop off your thumb onto the needle

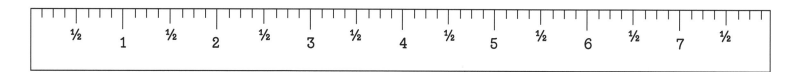

Pull the loop into place. It's now called a stitch.

The pattern you are following will tell you how many stitches to cast on. Once they are all on the needle, you begin knitting.

Continue casting on loops until you have the right number of stitches on the needle

How to Make a Knit Stitch:
Hold the needle with the cast-on stitches in your left hand and an empty needle in your right. Poke the right needle point into the first

stitch, going from front to back, crossing the right needle behind the left to make an X. Then wrap yarn under and over the right needle, and use the needle point to pull it forward through the stitch to make a new loop. The loop will be on the needle in your right hand.

Push the needle through the stitch, from front to back. Then wrap the yarn strand over the top of the needle, and down between the needles.

Pull the yarn through the stitch with the right needle. Slide it off. The new stitch is on the right needle.

It may help you to remember the steps to each stitch by repeating the following as you work: poke—wrap around—pull through—slide off. There are some rhymes that make it fun to remember:

"Under the fence,
Catch a sheep.
Back we come,
Off we leap."

And another:

"In through the front door,
Around the back.
Out through the window,
And off jumps Jack."

Keep making knit stitches until you reach the end of the row. Now all the stitches are on the *right* needle. Switch hands, putting the needle full of stitches in your left hand, and begin working another row of knit stitches. That's all there is to it. You are knitting!

Bind Off: When you're ready to quit knitting the piece, you'll *bind off* the stitches on the knitting needle. To bind off, knit 2 stitches.

Knit 2 stitches onto the right needle

With the left needle, lift the first stitch you made over the second stitch and lift it off the right needle.

Use the left needle to slip the first stitch you made over the second. Slide it off the needle. Only one stitch remains on the right side.

Knitting started in North Africa and the Middle East, then moved to Europe and Asia. It spread during the Middle Ages as sailors and traders taught others how to do it. At first most knitters were men. Later, women and girls started. It was a good way to make money without buying much equipment.

Men trained to become master knitters who got recognition for their skills—and better pay for their knitting work. To become a master knitter in 1600 (the 17th century), it took three years of practice knitting, three years of internship with master knitters, then 13 weeks spent making a final project. The final project was the masterpiece. The knitter created a final project by making these items as perfectly as possible:

A large knitted carpet with flowers, birds, and animal designs.
A knitted beret hat, which was then washed and felted.
A knitted wool shirt. (People didn't wear sweaters then; they are a more recent creation.)
A knitted pair of stockings with a fancy design on the side of the ankle, called a clock.

If the work was done well, he was admitted to the local knitters' guild. He could sell his knitted items for better prices and could someday have his own shop with apprentices to help him fill orders.

When knitting machines became popular in the mid-1800s, knitting by hand became a hobby. The days of the guilds were over.

Pull the second stitch you made through the first stitch. This is one stitch bound off. Keep the other stitch on the needle, and knit another stitch. Pull the first stitch over the one you just made, and lift it off the needle.

Knit another stitch. Slip the first stitch over it and slide it off the right needle.

Keep going until only one stitch remains on the needle. Then cut the working yarn and pull the yarn tail through the last loop you made. Tug it tight. This knot at the end will keep your piece from unraveling.

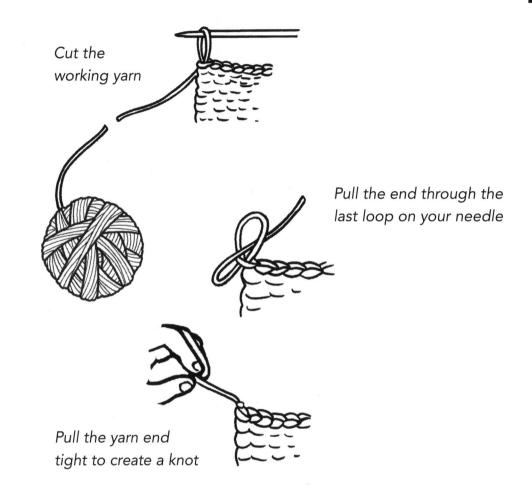

Cut the working yarn

Pull the end through the last loop on your needle

Pull the yarn end tight to create a knot

Headband or Ear Warmer

Many people make a square pot holder as their first knitting project. You can make that using these directions, of course. But why not make a longer shape—a rectangle—even longer to wrap around your head, and have a headband? It's just as easy as a pot holder, and looks a lot better on you!

Materials

Yarn, medium weight, or worsted weight
Knitting needles, size 8, 9, or 10
Yarn needle
Scissors

♣ Cast on 12 stitches. Your beginning slip-knot loop counts as the first stitch, so you'll need to cast on 11 more after the knot. Knit every row in knit stitch. Keep knitting row after row until the fabric is long enough to wrap around your head.

It should be snug, so it stretches a little to fit. When the band is long enough, bind off. Place the two short ends even with each other. Thread the yarn needle with matching yarn and stitch the ends together. Clip the end of the yarn about 3 inches long. Knot the yarn by pulling the end through the last loop. Pull tight and clip the end or weave it into the stitches to hide it.

12 stitches wide

Make it long enough to fit around your head

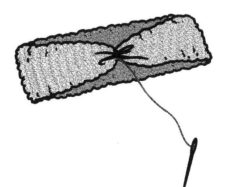

Stitch the ends together. Pull stitches tight to gather.

To make a "bow-tie" headband, pull the yarn tight after you sew the ends together. It will gather the ends to pucker. Knot the yarn securely. Then, wrap matching yarn around the center to cover the gathered section. It will look like it has been tied in a bow when you put it on your head. To decorate your headband, sew a few crocheted flowers (see page 114) on one side. Or you can stitch on a large button.

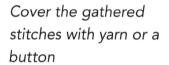

Cover the gathered stitches with yarn or a button

Knit Leg Warmers

Leg warmers are easy to make, look neat, and show off colorful yarns and stitches. It's usual to make both warmers the same, but you could try different colors if you like. To make striped warmers, change yarn colors at the end of a row. Tie on the new color and knit as many rows as you like, then switch colors. Always tie on the new yarn at the end of a row so the knot will be hidden in the seam when you sew the sides together.

Materials

Yarn, medium or worsted weight
Knitting needles, size 13
Scissors
Yarn needle

❧ Begin by casting on 30 stitches, with your slipknot counting as stitch 1. Work the entire first row in knit stitch. Turn (hold the needle with all the stitches in your left hand and the empty needle in your right) and continue working in knit stitch for each row. Knit stitch, done row after row, is called garter stitch, and it makes a stretchy fabric that looks good on both sides.

Keep knitting until the rectangle is as long as you like. Most leg warmers reach from the knee to the ankle, plus a little extra length

to make them slouchy. When you are satisfied with the length, bind off the stitches. Clip the yarn, leaving a tail about 20 inches long. Thread the tail end onto a yarn needle. Fold the rectangle in half the long way and stitch the edges closed. Done! Now make another,

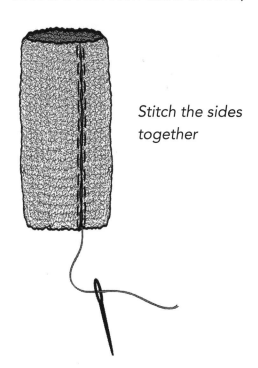

Stitch the sides together

with the same number of cast-on stitches and rows so they match.

If you find your warmers turned out a bit saggy at the top, weave a length of yarn (or some cord you made by finger knitting, page 50, or spool knitting, page 53), through the top row of stitches. Pull up to fit and tie securely. Why not add some tassels (see page 67) for even more style?

Warmers too loose?
Thread yarn through the top and
tie tight—add tassels, too.

Knit a Bag

Materials

Yarn
2 knitting needles, size 8, 9, or
    10
Scissors
Yarn needle

❧ Cast on 15 stitches. Working with the knit stitch, knit the first row. Keep knitting row after row until the piece is at least 8 inches long. Bind off and knot the last stitch.

Thread the needle with a length of matching yarn. Knot the end of the thread. Fold the knitted piece with the short edges together. Stitch down both sides, and knot the thread to secure it.

To make a handle, use a cord you made from the finger knitting project (page 50). Or you can braid a handle: Cut three pieces of yarn, each 18 inches long. Knot

the three together at one end. Close the knot in a drawer to hold it. Braid the three strands by following this pattern: left side over center, right side over center, and so on.

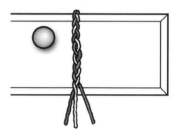

Braid a handle

Continue until you come to the end of the three pieces of yarn. Knot securely. Use the yarn needle and yarn to stitch both ends of the handle to the bag.

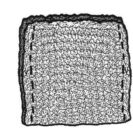

Stitch the handle to the sides of the bag

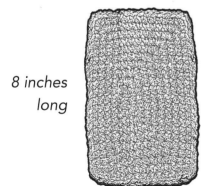

15 stitches

8 inches long

Fold and stitch both sides together

↙ *Fold*

Tasseled Scarf

A knitted scarf is a fashion classic. Guys, gals, even your favorite canine friends like to wear them. To make a simple scarf look very clever, add some tassels. Here's how:

Materials

Yarn, medium or worsted weight
Knitting needles, size 8 to 11
Scissors
Yarn needle
Cardboard, 3 inches by 5 inches

❖ Cast on 15 stitches. Begin knitting (knit stitch), continuing row after row until the scarf measures about 36 inches long. Try it on to be sure the length is what you want. Bind off the stitches, clip the working yarn, knot the end of the yarn, then hide the tail in the stitches.

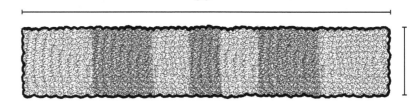

36"

15 stitches

Make two tassels, one for each end. Before you sew them in place, fold the corners at the ends of the scarf to the center, then sew the tassel over the center to hold the tassel and the ends in place.

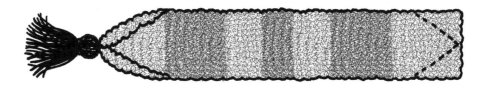

Fold corners to center, sew tassel in place

Make a Tassel

Using a piece of cardboard 3 inches by 5 inches, wind yarn around the cardboard the long way 50 times. Cut an 18-inch-long piece of yarn and slip it under the loops at the top of the cardboard. Pull it very tight and tie a square knot in the middle of the piece of yarn. With scissors, cut the loops apart at the other end of the cardboard.

Remove the cardboard. Cut a 6-inch length of yarn and wrap it tight twice around the tassel about 1 inch from the top. Knot it securely.

Thread a yarn needle with the two lengths of yarn hanging from the tassel and stitch it onto the scarf end, folding in the corner edges to the center of the scarf as you work. Make a second tassel and sew it to the other end of the scarf.

Slip yarn through loops at the top and tie a secure knot

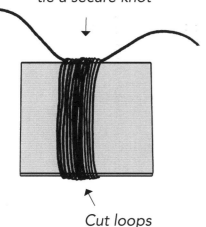

Cut loops

Thread the yarn ties onto a yarn needle

Tassel Doll

It's easy to turn a tassel into a little pocket pal. Make several in different colors. Glue on bits of felt or fabric for hats, shawls, belts, or whatever you can think of.

Materials

Yarn
Cardboard, 3 inches by 5 inches
Scissors
Felt or cloth scraps (optional)

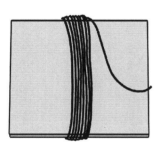

Wind yarn around the cardboard

Tie at one end

Divide and tie at the other end

♣ Wind the yarn around the cardboard the long way about 50 times. More yarn will make a fatter doll; less will make a thinner one.

Thread a short piece of yarn through all the loops on one end and tie a knot. Divide the loops into two equal groups at the other end. Thread through and knot lengths of yarn tightly around each group.

Gently slip the loops off the cardboard. Roll a short length of yarn into a ball and push it inside the top part, just below the knot, to fill out a head. Knot a small piece of yarn underneath it for a neck.

Wind about 25 yarn loops around the cardboard width-wise and tie a knot at each end to make arms. Slip it off

Tie yarn to make a head

the cardboard. Slip this arm section through the body, under the neck. Make sure the arms stick out evenly from each side and push it up close to the neck. Tie pieces of yarn crosswise around the body underneath the arms to hold the arms in place. Tie a waist, too. That's it! Make simple clothes from felt or cloth scraps if you wish.

Slip the arm section inside

Tie yarn to hold the chest and waist

Comfy Slippers

Knitting socks is a bit difficult for beginners, but slippers are easy. And slippers are a lot more useful because you can wear them every day.

Materials

Ruler

Yarn, bulky weight (or use 2 strands of worsted weight as if they were one strand)

Knitting needles, size 6

Yarn needle

Scissors

❖ Measure the length of your foot and write it down. Subtract 1 inch. That will be the measurement to follow for the length of the slipper. Because knitted fabric is stretchy, you want it to be shorter than your foot so it will stretch a bit to fit and not be too loose.

Cast on 20 stitches. (For an adult size, cast on 30 stitches.)

20 stitches

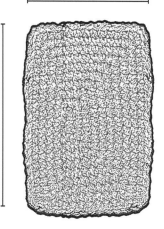

Your foot length less 1 inch

Knit every row (*garter stitch*). Keep knitting until the piece is as long as the measurement you figured out earlier (your foot's length minus 1 inch).

Bind off the stitches. Thread the yarn needle with a length of yarn about 18 inches long. Fold the rectangle in half lengthwise. Stitch one short end, using whip-stitch seams and making three stitches in one spot to secure the top edge. Clip yarn.

On the other end, use a threaded yarn needle and make straight stitches, about ½ inch long, along the edge.

Stitch along one end

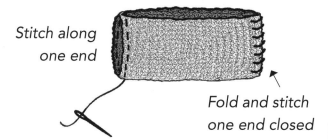

Fold and stitch one end closed

Pull the yarn tight to bring the edges together, creating the toe of the slipper. Make three small stitches next to each other to secure the gathers that make the toe.

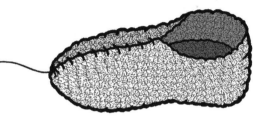

Pull the stitches tight to make the toe. Stitch the top together to fit your foot.

Sew the seam across the long edge with whip stitches, running from the top of the toe, but don't sew all the way across. Leave a hole big enough for your foot to fit into. You should try it on to make sure it's not too tight or loose. Secure the yarn with three small stitches, then cut the yarn.

That's it! You can turn the slipper inside out so the stitched areas are hidden inside.

Make another, just like the first. Decorate them by sewing on buttons, bows, crocheted flowers, pom-poms, or whatever suits you.

Nonslip Slippers

Slippers can do just that: slip. *Slippery footwear can be dangerous, so why not add a touch of grip to the bottoms to make them easier (and safer) to get around in?*

ADULT SUPERVISION REQUIRED

Materials

Newspapers

Plastic paint for decorating fabric, or clear silicone caulk sealant (Silicone caulk is sold in hardware stores for use on windows, doors, or kitchen and bath areas.)

Small bowl of water

❧ Work on a newspaper-covered surface. Use the same technique whether working with fabric paints or silicone caulk. Both come in squeezable containers.

Squirt the caulk over the sole of the slipper, making wavy lines. Wet your fingertips and gently flatten and smooth the lines until the entire sole is covered. It won't stick to your fingers if they are wet. Let it dry thoroughly. The time needed for drying is noted on the tube. Give it a little bit longer than required to be sure the silicone or paint is cured and won't come off the slippers when you wear them.

The slippers can be laundered by hand in cool water (if you used wool yarn), or warm water if the yarn is synthetic.

Squirt caulk on the slipper sole

Use wet fingertips to spread the caulk evenly over the sole. Let dry 24 hours.

KID WITH A CROOK
Crocheting

*C*rochet (pronounced "cro-SHAY") is a French word that means "hook." Crochet work is done by looping a strand of yarn with a tool that looks like a knitting needle with one hook-shaped end.

Crochet was invented by nomadic tribes in Africa and Asia. They used a crochet stitch now called Tunisian crochet, which is made with a crochet hook that has a long handle.

In the 1700s, people called crochet work "shepherd's knitting." Boys who spent the day watching the sheep flock while they grazed often crocheted so they could accomplish something and keep from getting bored.

Crochet can be done with small hooks and fine thread to make lace, or with large hooks and strips of rope to make rugs. It is faster than knitting, and it's harder for the work to fall off the needles, because you're only working with one tool and one loop at a time.

Learn to Finger Crochet

*I*t's lots of fun and very interesting to try making fabric with only your hands and yarn. That's what our ancestors did long ago as they sat and knotted fishing nets, then moved on to using stick tools and eventually knitting, weaving, and crocheting.

Materials

Just yarn and your fingers!

♣ In this project, you'll be pulling loops through other loops, using one continuous piece of yarn. You can do it with only your fingers, but once you get the hang of it, you'll probably want to move on to regular crocheting with a special hook tool. Finger crochet can be fun and easy; you can pick it up anywhere and make anything that has a square or rectangle shape, like coasters, washcloths, or scarves. Or you can fold and sew the edges together to make ponchos, bags, scarves, pillows, leg warmers, mitts, and boot covers.

Start by making a chain. You'll need to tie a slipknot in the end, making the first loop, then pull one loop through that and continue until it's as long as you want your project to be. For a scarf, a chain of 21 stitches works well. That will create a chain of 20 stitches, plus one for turning.

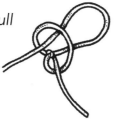

Make a slipknot. Pull a loop through the loop.

Continue pulling loops through loops.

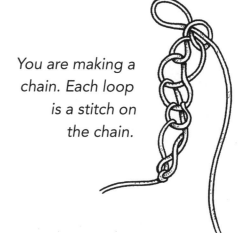

You are making a chain. Each loop is a stitch on the chain.

Once you have the chain completed, begin the first stitch. Keeping your index finger in the last loop, poke your other index finger through the chain loop that's next to the last one, to pull it open enough so you can pull a loop of yarn through both that loop and the loop that's on your right index finger. Hold the new loop on your finger, and repeat to create a new loop.

Continue working by pulling a new loop through both the next loop on the chain and the one on your finger, until you reach the end of the chain. Then chain one more loop, which will help start the next

Hold a loop on your index finger while poking through the next stitch. Two loops on your finger now.

row easily. Turn the piece over and continue pulling new yarn through each stitch as you work across the next row.

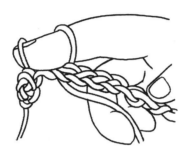

Pull working yarn through both of the loops on your finger

That makes one loop on your finger. Repeat the process to make the next stitch.

At the end of each row, make one new extra chain for turning. As you work, be careful to pick up and pull through all the chains on

the row. You should stop at the end of each row and count to be sure you still have the number you started with, in this case 20 (you cast on 21, with that extra one for turning). When you are finished with your crocheted piece and it's as long as you want, clip the yarn about 3 inches from the last stitch and tie a knot to secure it and keep the piece from unraveling.

Tips:

+ Use a medium-weight yarn—not too thin and not too thick. Worsted weight is easiest.

+ For beginners, it's easier to use multicolored yarn, because the colors change along each row. It will help you identify the stitches more easily—and it's more interesting to work with.

+ It's OK to unravel the work as you go if there is an area that looks odd or poorly done. Just pull the working yarn to pull the stitches out until you get to where you want to restart. It's called frogging your work. Don't be discouraged if you need to frog your work now and then.

+ Work loosely. It's easy to pull the yarn too tight because you don't have a crochet hook to hold the tension. Be careful when you pull new working yarn to make loops; don't pull the last loop you made too tight.

Finger Crochet Scarf

You can make an entire scarf with just yarn and your bare hands! It's simple to do; just start with a worsted-weight yarn.

♣ Begin with a slipknot, then, using only your fingers, make a chain 20 loops long.

Working into the second loop from the last one, pull it open and work a single-crochet stitch. It's easiest if you make sure not to twist the yarn, just make loops and pull them through each other. Continue to the end of the row. Chain one loop, then turn and work in the loop next to that one, and continue down the row.

Keep going, being sure to chain an extra loop for turning at the end of each row.

Count stitches now and then to be sure you aren't skipping any, as the pull from your hands is uneven without a crochet hook, and you may pull stitches closed and not see them.

Continue working the rectangle until it's as long as you like.

Nice work! Now head for the hook, if you want to move onto more elaborate designs.

Sculpt a Hook Handle

Crochet is done with a hooked tool that fits in one hand. The size of the hook varies, depending upon how large you want the stitches to be. Very tiny hooks and thin thread are used to make lace. Large hooks and thick yarn called roving are used to make very bulky items.

Crochet hooks are numbered, and patterns will suggest the size of hook the pattern was designed for. Since people around the world crochet, the sizes on hooks can be in alphabet letters (US sizes) and metric measurements (other countries).

You can make your crochet hook look bright and artistic by wrapping it in colorful polymer clay. Yours will be one-of-a-kind, not just a plain metal hook. It will also be easier to use and your work will go faster.

Ergonomics means design for comfort and function. With a thick clay handle on your crochet hook it will become more ergonomic and built especially to fit your hand.

ADULT SUPERVISION REQUIRED

Materials

Polymer hardening clay, either oven-bake or air-dry, about 2 ounces

Metal crochet hook (Do not use a plastic or wooden hook, since these will be destroyed in an oven.)

Oven and baking pan

Note: before you start, write down the size of the hook you will be covering. When your handle has cooled, write the size on the end with a permanent marking pen.

❧ Choose one color of polymer clay, or mix several to get a striped or marbled effect. Pinch off pieces until you have the amount you want, then wrap the rest of the clay in plastic wrap so it won't dry out. You can use it to make more handles, or make some buttons or beads.

Blend colors and roll clay into shape

Roll the clay pieces together into a smooth, hot-dog shape. Lay the metal hook handle onto the clay and wrap the clay around the metal, smoothing it together so it all blends. Press the clay firmly against the hook handle to push out air bubbles so it will be solid after baking.

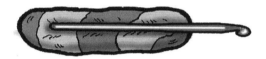

Press clay firmly around hook. Wrap it all around and smooth the edges.

Hold the hook in the hand you crochet with and press your fingers and thumb lightly into the clay so it shapes to your hand. Crochet a few stitches to be sure it will be comfortable.

Place the hook in a baking pan. Bake at 275°F for about 1 hour and 15 minutes. (Follow directions on your clay package if they differ.) Let it cool before touching.

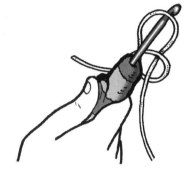

Crochet a few stitches with the handle, pressing your fingers into it to make good impressions in the clay. Bake as directed on the clay package.

Chain Up

You'll start crochet projects with chain stitches, made by looping yarn through itself and pulling it through with the hook. The length of the chain depends upon the project, so be careful to make the chain the proper length. Then you'll work stitches into those chain stitches to build the project.

Materials

Yarn
Crochet hook

♣ Make a slipknot near the end of the yarn.

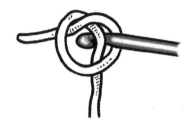 

Start with a slipknot

Slip the hook into the loop and begin pulling stitches through. Hold the hook as if it were a pencil or a dinner knife, whichever is more comfortable to you. Wrap yarn over the end of the hook, catch it with the hook and pull through the loop that's left on the hook. You made one chain stitch. Now make another, and watch the chain grow.

Make a chain

Chain-Stitch Necklace

Materials

Yarn
Clear tape
Pony beads, about 20
Crochet hook, size G, H, or K
(4 mm, 5 mm, or 6.5 mm)

String the beads onto the working yarn

Slip a bead into place and chain it in position

♣ Wrap the end of the yarn with tape so it will thread easily through the center of the beads without unraveling. Thread the beads onto the yarn, in a pattern or randomly.

With the beads strung on the yarn, go back and add chain stitches. Tie a slipknot on the tail end of the yarn and begin making chain stitches. Make 3 chain stitches, then work a bead into the next stitch. Do that by making a chain stitch with a bead on the yarn, picking up the yarn behind the bead with the hook, then into the next chain stitch. The bead is caught in the chain. Make 6 chain stitches, then add another bead. Keep the pattern of chaining 6 and adding a bead, or make up your own design. When the necklace is as long as you like, make 3 more chain stitches, then slip the yarn through the first chain you made, and pull a loop through the chain that's on the hook. Clip the yarn about 3 inches long and pull the end through the last loop to make a knot.

Chain a Lanyard

*L*anyards are very handy for holding house keys, name tags, or whistles. Make one for yourself and another for an adult who needs to wear ID cards to work.

Materials

Medium (worsted) or thick (bulky) weight yarn
Crochet hook, size I (5.5 mm) or larger
Scissors
Metal ring or large paper clip

❧ Start with a yarn tail about 6 inches long, then make a slipknot over your hook. Crochet a chain 30 inches long. Cut a yarn tail 6 inches long. Slip the cut end through the last chain stitch you made and pull tight to create a knot.

Slip the chain through a metal ring or large paper clip. Overlap the ends of the chain together with the other side of the chain loop as shown and wrap tightly with a length of yarn. Knot securely.

Wrap yarn securely to hold

Slip a ring over the chain. Overlap the ends.

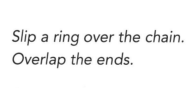

Braided Chain Bracelet

Chains are so much fun to make, you'll quickly have lots of them. What to do with all those chains? Braid them together to make a bracelet—or two.

Materials

Yarn
Crochet hook, size F (3.75 mm) or larger
Scissors
Button

❦ Start with a yarn tail about 6 inches long, then make a slipknot over the hook. Crochet a chain about 8 inches long. Cut the working yarn 6 inches from the last chain. Pull it tightly through the last chain stitch you made to make a knot. Set aside, and make two more chains the same length.

Knot the three chains together where the yarn tails begin. Braid the three chains together. You can slip the knotted end under a heavy book or inside a drawer to hold it securely while you braid. When you get to the end of the chains, knot the ends together.

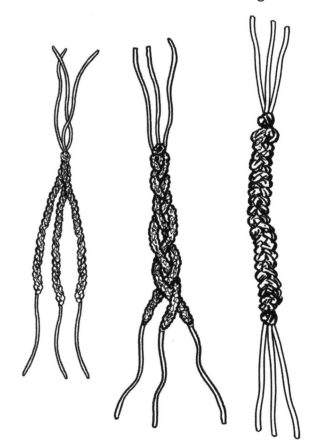

Fasten a button to one end by threading one of the yarn tails through the button holes, then knotting securely. Trim the yarn tails on the button end. To wear, slip the button through the end of the braid, letting the yarn tails dangle.

Stitch a button on one end of the braid

Chain a Necklace

You can use crochet chains to make simple necklaces—just knot the ends and tie together. Here's a necklace that has more: fringe!

Materials

Yarn (medium to thick weight)
Crochet hook, size I (5.5 mm)
   or larger
Scissors
Lightweight cardboard,
   3 inches by 5 inches

♣ Crochet a chain as long as you want your necklace to be. It should be long enough to slip over your head easily. At the end of the chain, cut the yarn and pull the end through the last chain you made. Pull tight to create a knot.

Tie the ends together. That's it for the basic necklace. Now decorate it with fringe.

To make fringe, create a template from a piece of cardboard the size you want the fringe to be; 3 inches by 5 inches is a good size. Wrap the yarn around the cardboard about 10 times—not too tight— then cut the yarn along one edge.

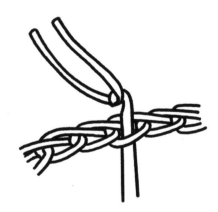

Wrap yarn around a piece of cardboard; then cut along one edge

To attach the fringe, poke the crochet hook through one of the stitches on the necklace chain. Fold a fringe piece in half to make a loop. Pull the loop through the chain with the crochet hook. Then

Use the hook to pull a loop through a chain

wrap the loose ends over the chain loop and pull the ends of the loop through itself. Keep the ends even and pull tightly. That makes one piece of fringe! Attach as many pieces as you want, pulling each loop through a stitch in the chain. Trim the ends evenly with scissors if needed, when you are finished.

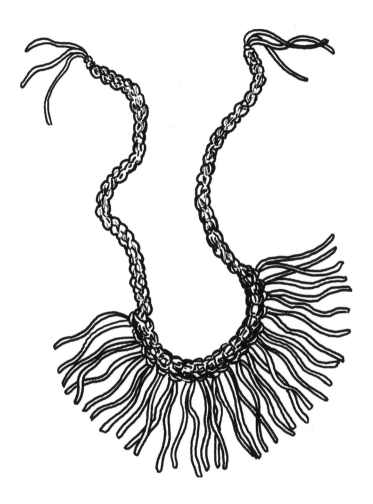

Pull the ends of the yarn loop through the loop to make fringe

Crochet Stitches to Know

Crochet stitches are made by pulling loops through loops. Here are the basic stitches you'll need to get started making more advanced crocheted projects. Patterns and instructions for crochet projects usually refer to the stitches with letters. You can learn this code easily. If a pattern tells you to make 4 dc, it means make 4 double-crochet stitches.

For all of these stitches, you'll be working from a chain you have already made. Skip one stitch and insert the hook into the second stitch away from the one on the hook. When you finish a row of stitches, make an extra chain stitch (ch 1). Keep your hook in the chain and turn your work over so you can crochet back across the tops of the stitches you just made. That extra "turning chain" will help keep the project the right shape.

For more information about how to learn crochet, you can go to the Craft Yarn Council website: www .craftyarncouncil.com.

slipknot

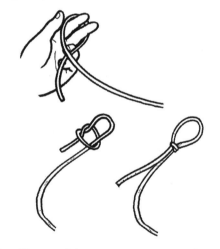

You'll use this to start any project. It fastens the yarn to the crochet hook. Wrap a loop around your fingers; then slip another yarn loop through the first loop. Put the hook through the loop and pull the yarn end to tighten. Think of the slip-knot loop on the hook as a stitch.

single-crochet (sc)

This is the basic crochet stitch. Insert the hook into the stitch, wrap the yarn over the hook, and pull up a loop. There will be two loops on the hook. Wrap the yarn over the hook again and pull it through both loops on the hook. One loop (the new stitch) will remain on the hook.

Slip the hook into the stitch. Wrap yarn over the hook. Pull a new loop through the stitch.

Now two loops on the hook

Wrap yarn over the hook again and pull through two loops. The new loop is now the first single-crochet stitch.

double-crochet (dc)

Wrap the yarn over the hook. Insert the yarn into the stitch, and wrap the yarn over the hook again. (If you're working the double-crochets into a chain row, make the first dc in the fourth chain from the hook.) Pull the yarn through the stitch. You'll have three loops on the hook. Wrap the yarn over the hook again and pull it through

two loops. Then wrap the yarn over the hook once more and pull it through the last two loops. You'll have one loop left on the hook.

Wrap yarn over the hook and slip the hook through the fourth chain from the hook

Pull a loop through and you will have three loops on the hook

Wrap yarn over the hook and pull through two loops on the hook

Wrap yarn over the hook again and pull through the two loops. One loop remains on the hook. Your double-crochet stitch is made!

half-double-crochet (hdc)

Wrap the yarn over the hook. Insert the hook into the stitch. (If you're working the half-double-crochets into a chain row, make the first hdc in the second chain from the hook.) Wrap the yarn over the hook and pull it through the stitch. Wrap the yarn over again and pull the yarn through all three loops on the hook.

Wrap yarn over the hook. Insert the hook into a stitch.

Wrap yarn over the hook again.

Pull a loop through the first stitch. Wrap yarn over the hook again and pull a loop through all three loops on the hook.

Easy-Peasy Bookworm Bookmark

This project uses all the basic skills: chain stitch, single-crochet stitch, and double-crochet stitch, as well as ending with a knot and tying off. It only takes a few yards of scrap yarn.

Materials

Yarn, medium or worsted weight
Crochet hook, size G (4 mm)
Scissors
Plastic eyes and glue or perma-
nent fine-point marker

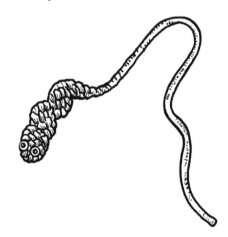

❧ Chain 63 stitches. Make 3 single-crochet (sc) in the second chain from the hook. Make all three stitches into the same stitch. Make 2 double-crochet (dc) in each of the next 12 chain stitches.

Work a single-crochet in the next two chain stitches.

Cut the working yarn about 6 inches long. Pull the end through the last loop on the hook. Pull it tight and it will knot securely. Trim the end or weave it inside the stitches in the project to hide it.

Make 3 single-crochet stitches in the second chain from the hook

3 sc in one chain

2 dc in next 12 chains

Your bookworm will look like this as you work along the chain. Cut the yarn and pull through the last single crochet to create a secure knot.

2 sc   *2 dc in 12 chains*   *3 sc*

Shape the worm with your fingers so it twists and curls into a worm shape with a little open mouth. Glue plastic eyes on the head, or mark two eyes with a permanent fine-point marker.

Pet Collar or Friendship Bracelet

Why not make this project for your best friend—person or pet? A pet collar and bracelet are similar because both are a band that fastens. Don't forget to make one for yourself, too.

Materials

Yarn, medium or worsted weight, 4 to 6 yards

Crochet hook, size H (5 mm)

Yarn needle

One parachute snap fastener (available from craft supply stores)

❧ To make a pet collar, make a crochet chain long enough to go around your pet's neck plus about 4 inches. A chain of 40 stitches fits most cats; 60 stitches will fit a medium-size dog. A chain of 60 stitches will be about 16 inches long. Crocheted yarn will stretch, and the parachute fastener is adjustable, so it should fit even if measurements aren't exact.

Chain 60 stitches (or whatever length works for your pet). Make a double-crochet stitch (dc) in the second stitch from the hook. Continue making double-crochet stitches (dc) in each stitch of the chain. At the end of the chain, cut the yarn, leaving about 18 inches of yarn attached to the work. Slip the yarn end through the last stitch to knot it.

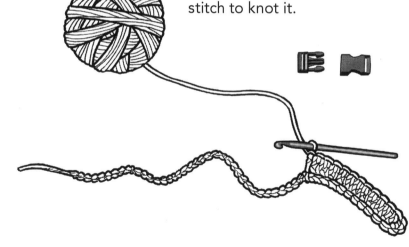

Work double-crochet stitches in each stitch of the chain

Thread the yarn end into the needle and stitch the end of the collar to the piece of the parachute snap fastener that has only one bar to sew onto. Stitch until no more yarn will fit into the fastener, then cut the yarn, tying the ends into a secure knot.

Now thread the other end of the collar into the other section of the fastener closest to the closure, then pull it through the outside opening, so it can be adjusted to fit your pet.

Stitch the band to the closures

To make a friendship bracelet, just make the starting chain shorter. Make the chain long enough to go around your wrist, plus 3 inches. Then double-crochet along the chain, stitch it to a parachute snap fastener, and give it to a friend!

Magic with Crochet Rectangles

A rectangle shape is easy to crochet and can be used to make lots of projects. You can make a plain rectangle or square and use it as a hot pad or coaster. Move on to making two of the same size and stitching them together to make pillows, bags, or a poncho.

It's fun to create unique items. Sometimes you'll be making a project, and suddenly it seems like a good idea to turn it into something else. Crocheted bags can become hats; mitts can become cell phone holders; belts become pet collars. Who knows what you can create?

Just keep your mind open to new ideas as you work.

The following projects are based on rectangle or square shapes. Some are small, others larger and more complex. They are all basically the same—crocheting in rows that are all the same length.

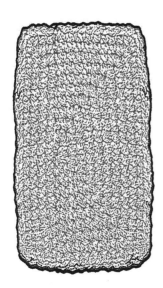

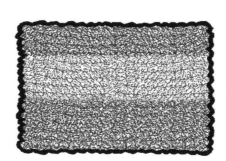

Bag

This simple bag can be used in many ways: eyeglasses case, phone cover, camera bag, or as a purse. Thick yarn (also called bulky or super bulky) will make a large, sturdy bag, while thinner sock-type yarn (also called fingering weight) will make a delicate bag.

Materials

Yarn, any weight
**Crochet hook, size H (5.0 mm) or
  larger**
Yarn needle

♣ Make a chain of 38 chain stitches. Work the single-crochet stitch into each loop of the chain. To make a single-crochet stitch, put the hook into the chain next to the hook, going under the two upper pieces of yarn. Loop yarn over the hook and pull it through the two pieces of the chain. Now you have two loops on the hook. Wrap yarn over the hook again and pull it through the loops on the hook. That's one stitch. Keep doing the same thing in every stitch of the chain. "Poke—wrap—pull through—wrap—pull through."

When you get to the last stitch in the row, turn the work and work another row of single-crochet. Keep working rows of the single-crochet stitch until the rectangle is about 5 inches long. Cut the working yarn and pull the tail through the last loop on the hook to bind off.

Poke the hook through the top two loops of the chain. Wrap yarn over the hook and pull through the two loops of the chain.

There will be two loops on the hook. Wrap yarn and pull it through both loops.

One loop will be on the hook. Start over in the next two loops of the chain.

38 stitches

5 inches

Thread the yarn needle with a length of yarn and stitch the side and bottom together to make a pouch.

Fold and stitch both sides together

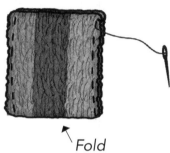

Fold

Crochet a long chain and sew the ends to your bag so you can wear the pouch over your shoulder, or tie it to your belt.

Crochet a chain handle and sew it to the sides

You may have read about George Washington Carver, a scientist and inventor who worked with peanut plants to create today's American peanut industry. Some say he "invented" the peanut. He worked for decades teaching and researching in biology and plant science, inventing hundreds—if not thousands—of uses for agricultural materials. Most people have not heard about his enthusiasm for textile arts. Carver was an expert at needle-work, crochet, basketry, spinning, and weaving. He especially liked making items from recycled and discarded materials. He explored the mathematical foundations of crochet and encouraged others to do handwork as well. Carver experimented with natural materials to dye fiber and yarn, such as using sweet potatoes to make lavender and orange colors. He used 28 different plants to dye fiber. He tried to figure out what the ancient Egyptians had used to make the brilliant blue paint color found in their tombs. Eventually, he discovered that clay soil was the source. He was recognized for his art work as a member of the Royal Society of Arts in England.

Necktie or Belt

A crocheted tie is easy to make and a great gift. You don't even have to know how to tie a necktie to wear this one.

Materials

Yarn, medium or worsted weight
Crochet hook, size H (5 mm)
Clip-on tie fastener (purchase at craft stores) or elastic braid, ½ inch wide, 18 inches long
Scissors

❧ Make a chain eight stitches long. Make a single-crochet (sc) in the second chain from the hook. Make single-crochet stitches in the rest of the row, ending up with six sc stitches in the row. Make a chain stitch, and turn to go back down the row you just did. Make single-crochet (sc) stitches in every stitch. Keep going, making each row of single-crochet with a chain stitch at the end for turning. Be sure to keep each row 6 sc stitches wide.

Continue working sc in every row until the necktie is about 28 inches long. It will be about 88 rows long. Clip the yarn and knot the end. Tuck the yarn's tail inside the crochet stitches to hide it.

Now you're ready to knot the tie and add the elastic, so it just pops on around the neck and tucks under a collar. Tie a loose slipknot with the necktie, about 8 inches from one end. Pull it into shape so it looks like a knotted necktie. Slip the elastic braid through the knot of the necktie. Stitch the ends of the elastic braid together, overlapping about an inch with the ends lying flat against each other.

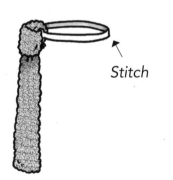

Stitch

If you would like to make a necktie that ties in a regular Windsor-style knot at the neck, make the necktie longer and omit the elastic loop. For a kid's tie, make the tie about 47 inches long. For an adult, it should be about 57 inches long.

To make a belt, follow the directions for the crochet necktie, but make the project long enough to fit around your waist plus about 2 inches. Buy a belt buckle or a parachute fastener at a fabric or craft store. Pull each end of the belt through the loops, fold it back, and stitch the ends in place securely.

You can also buy suspender parts at fabric and craft stores, and make a pair of suspenders following the same pattern. Just make the suspenders narrower. Start with a chain of 6 stitches, then work the rows in single-crochet.

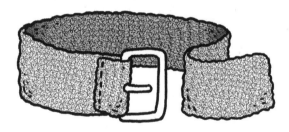

Stitch a buckle to one end. The prong can slip through the crochet stitches to fit.

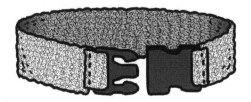

Stitch two parts of a parachute buckle to your belt

Jar Cozy Desk Organizer

Use a one-quart wide-mouth canning jar to make this useful holder for pens, pencils, crochet hooks, and knitting needles. It will decorate your room as it keeps things tidy. Mom or Dad would enjoy having one for their desk at work, too.

The project uses one yarn or a variety of short pieces, depending upon what you have. It's a perfect project for the Magic Yarn Ball (see page 116).

Materials

Yarn, worsted weight
Crochet hook, size H
(5 mm)
Yarn needle
Scissors
1-quart wide-mouth
canning jar

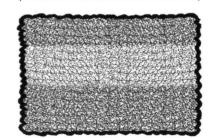

❧ Make a slipknot, then make 36 chain stitches.

Row 1: Work 1 single-crochet (sc) in the second chain from the hook and in the rest of the chains to the end.

Row 2: Chain 1, then work 1 sc in each of the sc stitches. Be sure to put the hook under both front and back loops of the single-crochets.

Row 3 through 18: Keep doing the same as row 2 until you reach the end of row 18. The piece should be tall enough to cover the height of the jar. If not, add rows as needed.

Row 19: Now you'll go backward. Chain 1, but do not turn the work. Work 1 reverse stitch in each stitch, coming back from left to right. A reverse stitch is the same as a single-crochet (sc) stitch, but the row is worked from left to right instead of from right to left. It will make a nice top edge for the project. If you find reverse stitches are too difficult, just make another row of single-crochet. Cut the yarn off and pass it through the last loop to bind off, leaving a tail about 12 inches long.

Start with 36 chain stitches

18 rows

Thread the yarn needle onto the yarn tail and stitch the cozy sides together. Put the right sides together, and stitch through the ends from the wrong side. Knot the yarn and clip the end when you're finished.

Turn the cozy right side out, and slide it up over the jar. You can add some buttons, ribbons, bows, or crochet a few flowers (page 114) if you want to add trim.

Boot Toppers

Sometimes called boot cuffs, this is a fun project that you can wear peeking out the top of your boots, or around the boot at the ankle. You'll want to make two alike, but you can use a variety of colors and yarns. What's even better, you'll learn to make fringe so your toppers have something extra special. If you want to turn them into leg warmers, just keep crocheting to make them longer.

Materials

Yarn, medium or worsted weight
Crochet hook, size N (9 mm)
Scissors
Yarn needle
Ruler

♣ To make a small cuff, chain 22, and it will be about 7 inches long. To make a larger one, chain 30 and it will be about 10 inches long.

Start by making a chain of 22 stitches (or 30 for large).

Make a row of single-crochet stitches (sc) starting in the second chain from the hook. Chain 1 and turn. Continue row after row, making sc stitches in each row and ending each row with a chain 1 for turning. Work for 16 rows. Cut the yarn about 18 inches long. Slip the yarn through the last stitch to create a knot. Thread the end of the yarn into the yarn needle. Fold the cuff in half the short way, with the sides meeting evenly. Stitch the ends together. Knot and clip the end of the thread.

Sew the sides together securely

Now the real fun begins, as you make fringe for decoration. Look at the Chain a Necklace project (page 84) to learn how to measure and cut the fringe pieces. You'll need the same number as the original chain (22 or 30). Fold each piece in half and use the crochet hook to slip the folded end through one of

98

the stitches along the edge. Pull the two ends of the yarn through the loop, being careful that the ends are even. Pull tight to secure the strand. Continue with each piece of yarn until the entire edge has fringe.

To wear, slip the un-fringed part inside your boot and fold the fringed edge over the top of the boot.

Pull loops of fringe through each stitch loop

Fold over the top of your boot

Hat

This hat is a lot like making the Jar Cozy Desk Organizer, but larger. It will take more time, but it will be well worth doing. Plus, this project has three different versions, so you can "choose your own adventure" as you decide what stitches you want to use.

Materials

Yarn, worsted weight
Crochet hook, size N (9 mm)
Yarn needle
Scissors
Measuring tape or ruler

♣ Make a chain 25 stitches long. (If you want to make a hat for an adult, make it 33 stitches long.)

Work a single-crochet (sc) in the second chain from the hook. Work the rest of the chain in single-crochet (sc).

Choose what stitch pattern you want to use for the hat:

- ✦ You can make every row in single-crochet stitches.

- ✦ You can make every row in double-crochet stitches.

- ✦ Be adventurous and alternate rows, doing one in single-crochet, the next in double-crochet.

At the end of the first row, chain 1 stitch and turn if you are doing single-crochet on the next row. Chain 2 stitches and turn if you are doing double-crochet stitches on the next row. You need that extra chain so you can turn and start a new row without pulling the yarn too tightly into the next stitch.

Whichever pattern you choose, continue it until your rectangle is 6 inches long. Then make a final row in single-crochet stitches to match

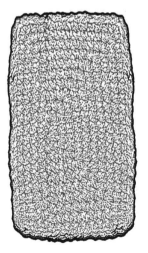

the one you started with. Clip and knot the yarn.

Fold the rectangle in half, inside-out, with the ends meeting evenly. Use the yarn needle and a length of yarn to stitch both sides together.

Try it on for size. If it is too loose, stitch it tighter at the sides.

Pull the two corners at the top fold to the center and stitch them together with a few stitches.

Now it's a hat! If you want to add a tassel, make one using the directions on page 67. Stitch the tassel through the center of the hat where the two corners meet.

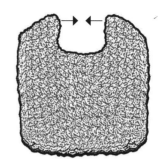

*Pull the corners
to the center*

*Stitch the corners
together*

Fold

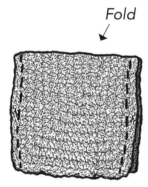

*Stitch sides, then turn
right side out*

*Add a tassel to
the top*

Hand Mitts

Gloves without fingers have been popular for centuries. They're quick to make because you don't have to make 10 little tubes for fingers. And your fingers are free to write, type, or crochet more projects. Here's a simple way to make mitts that works well for any worsted weight or bulky yarn. You don't need much yarn to make a pair, so it's a great way to use up odds and ends of yarn from other projects. If you use two colors of yarn, be sure they are worked in the same number of rows in both mitts. That will create a stripe effect. You can add crochet trim on the wrist, if you want.

Materials

Worsted weight or bulky yarn, in two colors to stripe
Crochet hook, size G (4 mm)
Scissors
Yarn needle

❧ You'll be making a square shape, then folding it in half and stitching the side closed, leaving an opening for your thumb. The instructions here may need to be altered, depending upon the size of your hand and how long you want the mitts to be. A square will make a mitt that ends at about the wrist.

Tie a slipknot at the end of the yarn and begin by making a chain 24 stitches long. Make a double-crochet in the fourth chain from the hook. The chains that you skipped count as the first double-crochet in the row. Double-crochet in each remaining chain stitch across. Work in the double-crochet stitch for about 9 rows, making 2 turning chains at the end of each dc row. Clip and tie the end.

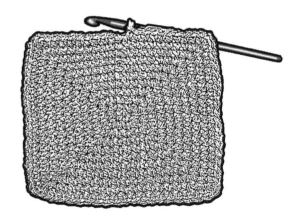

Crochet a square

Fold the mitt in half, stitching together with the yarn needle and matching yarn. Stitch halfway up the side, leave a thumb opening, then stitch the rest of the seam.

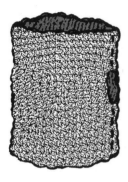

Fold and stitch the side. Leave an opening for the thumb.

If you want to add a border that looks like a wavy edge to the bottom of the cuff, insert your hook at the side seam and chain 2, then single-crochet in the next stitch. Chain 2 and double-crochet 4 times in the next stitch. Chain 2 and single-crochet in the next

stitch. Repeat the pattern all the way around: chain 2 and double crochet 4 times in the same stitch; then chain 2 and single crochet once. Chain 2, double crochet 4 times; chain 2, single crochet 1 time. Continue that pattern until you reach the end of the round. Knot and tie off.

One down! Whip out another and you're finished!

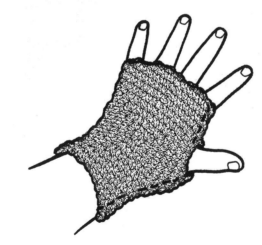

Mustache and Beard

These are fun to make, fun to wear, and when the weather is cold outside, will keep your face warm. Choose yarn that is the color of your hair, or try something unusual.

Materials

Yarn, worsted weight
Crochet hook, size K (6.5 mm)
Yarn needle or sewing needle
  and thread
Scissors

❧ Make a chain 23 stitches long. Make a double-crochet (dc) in the third chain from the hook. Keep making double-crochet (dc) stitches in the rest of the chain. At the end of the chain, chain 2 stitches and turn your work. The turning chain will be the first dc of the row.

Make the mustache by working 7 dc on the second row, then making a chain of 8 stitches. Skip 6 stitches from the last dc you made, and make a dc in the seventh stitch. Finish the row with dc stitches. Chain 2, turn, and dc across the row, making a dc stitch in each stitch, including the chain you just made in the center. That creates the opening for the mouth.

Continue with the rest of the beard, making a dc in every stitch, doing 2 chain stitches at the end of every row, then turning your work, before making the first dc of the next row. Keep crocheting until it's as long as

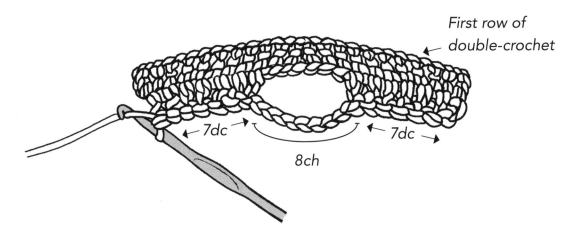

First row of double-crochet

←7dc→   ←7dc→

8ch

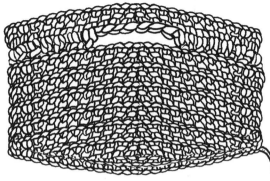

Keep working rows of dc until beard is as long as you want it

you want it to be. Clip the yarn and make a knot to end the beard. Make 2 chains, each 15 stitches long. Knot the ends and sew them to the sides of the beard, adjusting to fit. Wrap and knot a piece of yarn tightly around the center of the mustache section to pull it together for shape. It's ready to wear!

If you want to add long, flowing hair to the beard, cut lengths of yarn, fold them in half, and use the crochet hook to pull the loops through the crochet stitches of the beard. Pull the loop back to the right side of the beard with the crochet hook, and pull the ends of the yarn through the loop. Pull tight and it will stay secure. Trim the ends once you have finished adding the beard hair.

Wrap and knot yarn to create mustache

Sew chains onto the sides; slip them over your ears

Triangle Scarf

A triangle is easy to make. You'll start with short rows of crochet stitches, adding two stitches to each row. It will grow in size as you crochet each row. It takes less than a skein of yarn, so you can make one for yourself and another for a friend.

Materials

Yarn, worsted weight
Crochet hook, size I (5.5 mm)
Scissors

❧ Begin with a slipknot on the crochet hook. Then chain 4. Make a single crochet (sc) stitch in the second chain from the hook. Make single crochet (sc) stitches in the next 2 chains. You will have 3 stitches in that first row.

Make 1 chain stitch so you can turn and make a new row.

Make 2 single crochet (sc) stitches in the first stitch to start the row. Make 1 sc in each stitch across. Make 2 sc in the last stitch in the row. That will make the row 2 stitches longer than the previous row. Each row will grow by two stitches, as you add one stitch at the beginning and end of each row.

Continue working the same pattern: Chain 1 to start each row. Work single crochet (sc) stitches across each row, adding one extra sc in the first and last stitch of the row.

The triangle will grow larger. You can stop after six rows, and make the kerchief for a doll. Or keep going until the triangle sides are large enough to reach across your head from ear to ear.

Make the ties: At the end of the final row, continue without cutting the yarn. Make a chain 30 stitches

Add one stitch at the beginning and end of each row

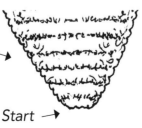

Start →

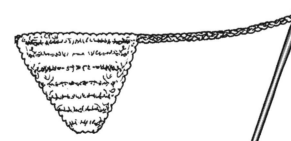

Make a chain to create the tie

long. Then start in the second chain from the hook and work single crochet (sc) stitches back over the chain to the scarf. When you reach the scarf, continue working single crochet stitches in each stitch across the scarf. At the other end of the scarf, make a chain 30 stitches long. Work single crochet (sc) in the chain, back to the scarf. Finish with 2 sc to secure the yarn. Clip the yarn, make a knot, and hide the yarn tail in the scarf stitches.

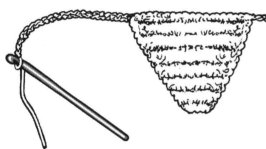

Work single-crochets in the tie chain, across the scarf. Continue a chain for the second tie. Single-crochet back on it and knot the yarn in the scarf.

Triangle Barefoot Sandals

*B*arefoot sandals are fun—they show off your crochet work and are quick to make.

Materials

Yarn, medium or worsted weight
Crochet hook, size I, J, or K (5.5 mm, 6 mm, or 6.5 mm)
Scissors

❧ This project is like the Triangle Scarf, with a twist. Start with a slipknot on your crochet hook and make 4 chain stitches. Make a single crochet (sc) in the second chain from the hook. Make single crochets (sc) in the next 2 chains. The row will have 4 stitches. Chain 1 to turn and start a new row. Make 2 sc stitches in the first stitch in the row. Continue making single crochet stitches down the row, making 2 sc stitches in the last stitch in the row. Continue that pattern: 1 chain to start a new row; 2 sc in first stitch, sc the row, 2 sc in the last stitch. Make seven rows in that pattern.

Do not cut the yarn, but make the first tie by making a chain 40 stitches long. Clip the yarn and pull the end through the last chain stitch to make a knot.

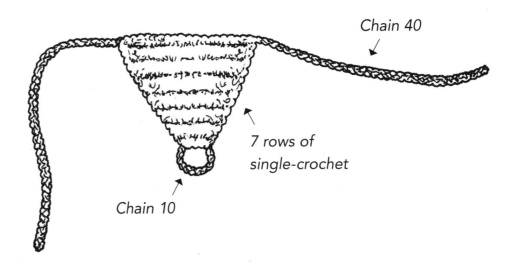

Chain 40

7 rows of single-crochet

Chain 10

Attach yarn to make the other tie. Slip the end of the yarn through a corner stitch on the triangle. Use the crochet hook to pull it through. Tie a knot. Make a chain 40 stitches long. Cut the working yarn and pull the tail through the last chain stitch to make a knot.

Now make the toe-piece. Tie the yarn on through one of the stitches at the bottom triangle point. Chain 10 stitches. Cut the yarn about 6 inches from the hook. Pull the tail through one of the stitches at the point of the triangle, then pull it through the last chain you made. Pull tight to make a knot.

Make another sandal just like the first. You can sew or glue some flowers to the top of the sandal. See page 39 for how to make Fork Flowers.

To wear your barefoot sandals, slip your second toe through the toe loop and tie the ties behind your ankle.

Slip the loop over your toe

Stretchy Hair Bands

rochet is fun because you can work in circles, making rounds very easily. You start from the center, working with one center chain or loop, then grow each round by adding more stitches. If you forget to add stitches as each round grows, the circle will not lie flat.

You can make ponytail holders or larger hair bands look special. Use the stretchy band as a base, then crochet in the round. You will work all around the center circle made of the band.

Materials

Stretchy ponytail holder or hair band
Yarn, worsted weight
Crochet hook, size G or H (4 mm or 5 mm)
Scissors

♣ Use a slipknot to fasten the yarn to the band. Work the stitches onto the band, working double-crochet (dc) stitches all around the band until you meet up with the first one you made.

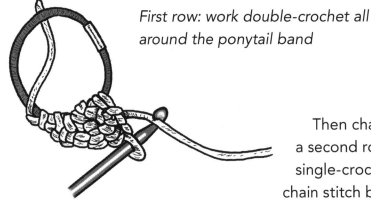

First row: work double-crochet all around the ponytail band

Then chain 3 stitches, and make a second round, this time using single-crochet stitches with one chain stitch between each one.

When you reach the chain 3 section you started the row with, make a slip stitch to join the ends. Make it by sliding the hook inside the first stitch you made, then pulling a loop through it and the loop on the hook. Then make a knot, and clip the end of the yarn.

Work a second row: Chain 3, sc in dc, chain 1, then sc in next dc. Chain 1, repeat. You'll make 1 chain between each sc.

Granny Squares

You can easily make granny squares, which are worked around a center circle, too. Granny squares are a crochet favorite. They can be made in different types of yarn, using any size hook. Make the squares as large or small as you want. One square can be made the size of a blanket by adding more rounds. Or you can make tiny squares with a pin and thread and use them as earrings.

Make as many squares as you need for a project, or as many as you can from your yarn supply—then decide what to make them into.

Materials

Yarn, any weight
**Crochet hook, size G, H, or K
    (4 mm, 5 mm, or 6.5 mm)**
Yarn needle
Scissors

♣ Work a granny square in rounds, not rows. You will start your stitches in the center and the square will get larger with each round. You can make the entire square the same color. Or try to make each round a different color, knotting and clipping yarns to join. Let's get started!

Begin with a chain 5 stitches long. Join the first stitch to the last with a slip stitch by slipping the end

of the hook into the first chain you made and pulling a yarn loop through it and the stitch on your hook to form a ring.

Now crochet stitches into the ring. Because you are making a square, you will need to make four corners on each round. Chain 3, then work 2 double-crochet stitches into the ring, working *around* the chains rather than *in* them. For this first cluster, the chain 3 counts as a double-crochet. Chain 2, and make another cluster of 3 double-crochet. For the next two clusters, work in a "chain 2, 3 dc" pattern until you have made four clusters of 3 dc. Chain 2 and slip stitch into the first chain 3 of that round. Look at what you did and you'll see it makes a little square.

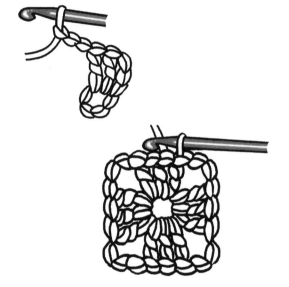

Work the next round by turning your work (flip the square over), so you can stitch into the last chain 2 space you made in the previous round. Chain 3, then work 2 dc into the chain space. The chain 3 counts as a dc, so you have made a cluster of 3 dc. Chain 2 and work

another 3 dc into the same space. You've made a corner. Chain 2 and make another corner in the next ch 2 space: 3 dc, ch 2, 3 dc. Continue until you have four corners made, each with two clusters of 3 dc separated by a ch 2 space. End with ch 2, then slip stitch into the top of the first chain 3 that started the round.

Turn over your work, and chain 3. You're ready to make a 3 dc cluster in the first ch 2 space. BUT now things change: you're working on sides, not corners. On the sides, work only 1 cluster of 3 dc in each space between clusters on the previous round. Work only 1 chain between clusters on the sides of the square. Continue making two clusters of 3 dc in the corner space and 2 ch between clusters on corners of the square.

So, starting with that ch 3 turn you just made (which counts as a dc), make 2 dc in the ch 2 space. Then ch 1 (because you are

working on a side) and make 3 dc in the corner space, ch 2, 3 dc in the same space, and continue the pattern. From here on, no matter how big you make your squares, you'll be doing the same thing:

- Ch 3 and turn your work at the beginning of each round.

- Make clusters of 3 dc in each space on the sides.

- Make ch 1 between clusters on the sides.

- Make two sets of 3 dc clusters with a ch 2 between clusters at the corners.

Make as many squares as you want, then lay them out on a table to create your project. Sew them together with a yarn needle and matching yarn. Place the right sides together, and stitch on the wrong side of the squares. Use your needle to pick through the stitches, pulling yarn through the loops of one square, then the other, until both are linked. Be sure you don't pull the yarn too tight or the squares will pucker along the seams. Knot and clip yarn ends.

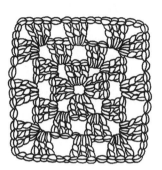

Make several squares, all the same size, and you can put them together to create lots of different projects.

Here are some ways to use granny squares:

- Sew two onto back pockets of jeans.

- Stitch six together, then stuff to make a ball and sew closed. Make two more and start juggling.

- Stitch three together in a ring and create a drink cozy.

- Six or more linked together make a scarf.

- Sew several together to make two equal-sized rectangles; then sew the rectangles together on the ends, making a poncho.

Sew squares to make two rectangles

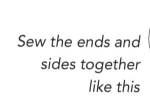

Sew the ends and sides together like this

You made a poncho!

Flowers

Crochet flowers are a really neat project you can do easily and use to decorate almost anything. You can make them with various sizes or weights of yarn and different sizes of crochet hook. That will make them larger or smaller than the directions here. Experiment a bit and make a bouquet of them!

Here are a few ways to make them:

Little Posies: The simplest to make, these flowers are about an inch across and have five simple petals. Use a size H crochet hook and worsted weight yarn. Tie a slipknot on the end of the yarn and begin by making 4 chain stitches. Work 1 single-crochet (sc) in the first chain stitch you made. That first stitch will be called the "ring." Chain 3 stitches. Work 1 sc in the

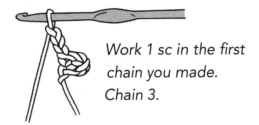

Work 1 sc in the first chain you made. Chain 3.

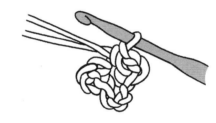

Work 1 sc in the ring. You made a petal. Make another: ch 3, 1 sc in the ring.

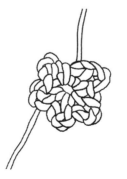

Make four more petals

ring, chain 3 stitches, then work 1 sc in the ring. Keep repeating the pattern of 1 sc in the ring, chain 3, three more times, until you have made five petals. Knot and clip the yarn, leaving a tail about 6 inches long so you can sew the flower onto a project.

Daisy Crochet Flower: Start with a slipknot. Chain 4. Slip stitch into the first chain you made. Now you have a ring. Work 9 single-crochet (sc) around the ring, working *over* the chains rather than *in* them. To work around the ring, insert the hook into the center of the ring, wrap yarn around the hook, then pull that loop back through the ring, leaving two loops on the hook. Wrap yarn around the hook again and pull it through both loops that are on the hook. That's one sc in the ring. Continue until you have 9 in the ring. Slip stitch into the first sc you made. Chain 8 stitches. Skip the first sc next to the chain and slip stitch into the second sc. You made a petal. Chain 8 again, skip one sc and slip stitch into the next sc. Work around until you have five petals. Cut the working yarn and slip it through the last stitch to create a knot.

9 sc in the ring

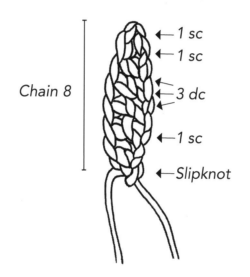

Make a petal: Chain 8 for each petal. Skip 1 sc, slip stitch into the next sc.

Quick Little Leaf: Use green yarn to make several leaves to use with your flowers. To make a leaf, chain 8. Make a sc in the second chain

from the hook. Make a sc in the next chain. Make a double-crochet (dc) in the next 3 chains. Make a sc in the last chain. Clip, knot, and tie off the yarn. You can leave a yarn tail long enough to stitch the leaves in place with a yarn needle later.

Chain 8   ← *1 sc*
← *1 sc*
← *3 dc*
← *1 sc*
← *Slipknot*

Twisty Vines: Flowers need leaves and stems—and vines. Working with green yarn, make a few of these vines to stitch in place with your flowers. Begin with a slipknot, then make a chain as long as you

want the vine to be. Start in the second chain from the hook, and single-crochet (sc) in every stitch of the chain. Cut the yarn, pull the end through the last loop to create knot. Clip the yarn.

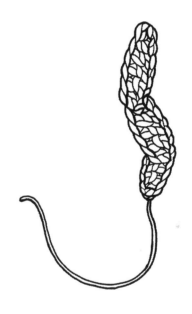

Magic Yarn Ball

If you or someone you know has a stash of bits and ends of yarns they haven't used, make a Magic Ball from it. As you knit or crochet with the yarn, it will change suddenly from one yarn to another, so you can't predict how your finished project will look. You won't be able to see all the colors because the yarn is wound in a ball. As you work with the yarn and the ball unwinds, new colors will appear—that's the magic.

Materials

Variety of yarns (All should have the same laundering methods—all hand wash, or all machine washable. Mixing may create problems when laundering a finished project.)
Scissors

❧ Gather up as much scrap yarn as you can. Set it out on a table and begin. Pull lengths of yarn in 2- to 3-yard lengths and knot the ends together. To create a color blending effect, link yarns that have similar colors. If it's a black and white blend, maybe link a white and tan blend, then choose a tan and orange one next, and so on. Or choose greens, one after another, until you choose a blue-green, then move into more shades of blue. Looking at the color wheel (page 118), you can link colors from the same family, then once in a while choose a piece that's a complementary color. For example, tie and roll up yellows, oranges, and tans, then choose a bright blue (complement to orange) for accent.

It's fun to invite friends to join you, making a party of it. Everyone brings their yarns and puts them out on the table. Then everyone walks around the table choosing yarns to add to their Magic Ball. After an hour or so, everyone should have a large ball of unusual colors and textures, ready for their next project.

The yarn color changes as you unroll and work on the project. When picking yarn to roll into a Magic Ball, choose colors that look good together.

COLOR, COLOR, COLOR
Dyeing

We love color—the brighter, the better. We admire rainbows in the sky after a rainstorm, and the brilliant coloring of flowers, birds, and fish. When people figured out how to add more color to their world, there was no holding back. For thousands of years, colors from plants, minerals, and even insects were used in dyes that colored fabrics and tinted paints, making life more interesting. Today we use chemicals, too, to create brilliant colors that last without fading or washing away.

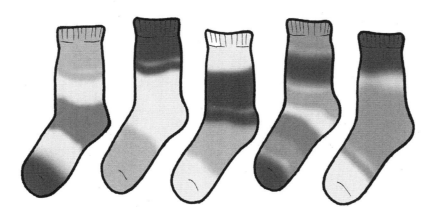

The Color Wheel

Color is important, and there are a few basic facts that all designers and artists must know, whether they are creating new automobiles, painting a portrait, or designing T-shirts. The color wheel organizes colors and shows how they can be mixed to make more colors. The color wheel was invented in the Middle Ages (1666) by Sir Isaac Newton—yep, the same person who discovered gravity.

The three basic colors, called primary colors, are red, yellow, and blue. Using them, all other colors are created. The three secondary colors are made by mixing primaries. The secondary colors are orange, green, and violet (also called purple). To help you remember how colors can be mixed to create new ones, make a color wheel of your own.

Materials

White paper plate
Pencil
Paints, crayons, markers, or pieces of yarn to fill in each triangle on the wheel: red, yellow, blue, orange, green, and violet

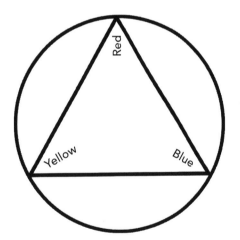

❧ On the white paper plate, draw a triangle that touches the edges of the plate. Mark the corners of the triangle with a pencil: red, yellow, blue.

Make another triangle, upside-down from the first, using a dotted line. The points of this second triangle will locate the secondary colors. Each secondary color goes between the colors that blend to create it. For example, yellow + blue make green. Label green between the primary colors of yellow and blue. Red + blue make violet, so label violet between red and blue. Red + yellow make orange, so put it between red and yellow. To create your color wheel, use paints, crayons, markers, or pieces of yarn or paper to fill in the color sections. Using paints, practice mixing colors that are next to each other on the wheel. Then try mixing colors that are directly across from each other on the wheel. Which blends make brown?

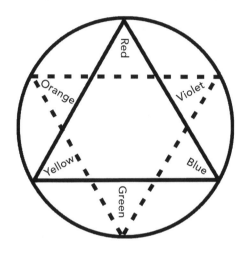

Colors next to each other on the wheel are in the same color family and go together nicely in any project. Colors that are opposite each other on the color wheel are called complementary colors. Putting them together in a project will make both colors seem brighter and add interest. Experiment with colors, finding your favorite combinations.

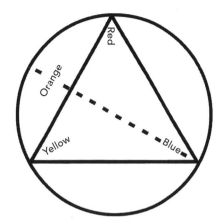

Complementary colors: Orange and blue are across from each other on the wheel, so they are complementary colors.

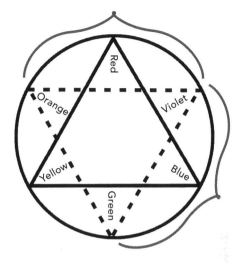

Color families: Violet, blue, and green are next to each other on the wheel, so they are in the same color family. Red, orange, and violet make up another color family.

The color pink is calming. It is used on walls in hospitals to make people feel more comfortable.

The colors yellow and orange make you hungry. Have you noticed any restaurants that use a lot of yellow or orange in their signs or decor?

Blue is the most popular favorite color worldwide. Purple is the second-most favorite color.

Most people like bright colors more than neutrals, such as gray or brown.

Spice Dyes

Dyes made from spices can be used to dye yarn or natural fabrics and clothing. A popular spice called turmeric is perfect for a pot of dye. Other spices that make great dyes are saffron, paprika, chili powder, and many others. Just look for vivid colors. Turmeric is found in most grocery stores and is actually very healthy for you to eat. It dyes wool or cotton a bright yellow, which can run from pale to dark, depending upon how much turmeric you use. Use less for a pastel, more for a solid hue.

ADULT SUPERVISION REQUIRED

Materials

White fiber (You can use wool or cotton yarn, T-shirts, socks, or just about anything that contains natural fiber. Polyester and acrylic won't hold the natural dye as well.)

Large pot

Water

Vinegar

Measuring cup

Measuring spoon

Powdered turmeric (found in the spice section of the grocery store)

Long-handled spoon

Stove

♣ Before starting any dyeing project, be sure to protect your workspace (a plastic shower curtain or large garbage bags will work), your clothing (wear an old shirt or apron), and your hands (use plastic gloves or put your hands in plastic sandwich bags). Dye will color things you don't want colored, too, so work carefully, and prepare everything before you start.

Put whatever you're going to dye in the pot and fill it with enough lukewarm water to cover. Add ½ cup of vinegar. Swish the fiber around to mix in the vinegar. Let it sit for about 20 minutes, until the fiber is thoroughly wet.

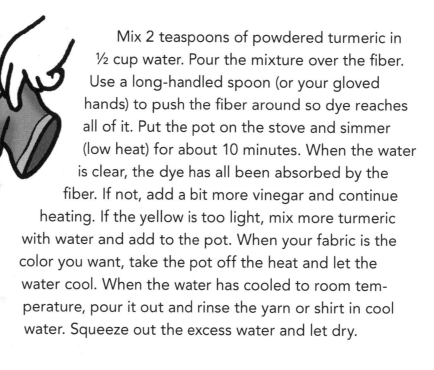

Mix 2 teaspoons of powdered turmeric in ½ cup water. Pour the mixture over the fiber. Use a long-handled spoon (or your gloved hands) to push the fiber around so dye reaches all of it. Put the pot on the stove and simmer (low heat) for about 10 minutes. When the water is clear, the dye has all been absorbed by the fiber. If not, add a bit more vinegar and continue heating. If the yellow is too light, mix more turmeric with water and add to the pot. When your fabric is the color you want, take the pot off the heat and let the water cool. When the water has cooled to room temperature, pour it out and rinse the yarn or shirt in cool water. Squeeze out the excess water and let dry.

Food Dyes

This is an easy way to color tiny amounts of yarn, or even Easter eggs. Because you are using the three primary colors (red, yellow, and blue), you can mix up lots of other colors too. Be sure to soak the yarn, felt, or fiber in water first, before using the dye.

ADULT SUPERVISION REQUIRED

Materials

White or light-colored yarn, felt, cotton balls, or wool (pre-soaked in water)

3 small glasses

6 tablespoons vinegar

1 teaspoon beet powder (sold in health food stores)

2 tablespoons fresh or frozen blueberries

Pinch of baking soda

1 tablespoon prepared mustard (you can use little condiment packets from restaurants)

Saucepan, strainer, spoons

Divide the vinegar between three small glasses, putting 2 tablespoons in each glass.

To make pink or red dye, mix 1 teaspoon of beet powder into ½ cup very hot water. When it's dissolved, pour it into one of the glasses with vinegar.

To make blue, put 2 tablespoons of blueberries into a small pan, add ½ cup water, and boil until the cooking causes the berries to split open. Stir in a pinch of baking soda. Strain the mixture and add the liquid to one of the glasses of vinegar.

For yellow, stir 1 tablespoon of mustard into ½ cup very hot water. Pour it into one of the glasses of vinegar.

Now you have all three primary colors. Dip pieces of wet felt, yarn, or wool into the cups of coloring. Try dipping in different colors or making two-tones. The blueberry dye will look reddish, but as it dries it will turn blue.

Here are some other foods you can use to make natural dyes:

- tea
- coffee
- onion skins

Drink Mix Dyes

You won't need vinegar when using drink mixes for dyeing because there is citric acid in the mix that will help to set the color so it won't wash out. You must also use heat, so you'll need access to a microwave or stove.

ADULT SUPERVISION REQUIRED

Materials

Wool or cotton yarn
Scissors
Large microwave-safe bowl (or a
  saucepan for the stove)
Water
Powdered drink mix, such as
  Kool-Aid (unsweetened)
Small glass or measuring cup
Microwave oven (or a stove)
Plastic wrap if using a microwave
Clothes hanger

❧ Decide how much yarn you want to color, then create small skeins to make it easier for the dye to soak into the fibers. Make the skeins of yarn by wrapping yarn around your arm, hooking it around your thumb and elbow. After a few wraps, slip it off and lay it flat on a table. Cut four small lengths of yarn, about 3 inches long. Tie them around the skein in different places to keep the skein from tangling while you are working with it.

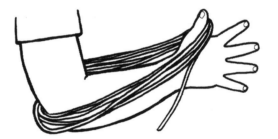

Wrap yarn around your elbow and hand

Tie the yarn loops into a skein in four places

Put the yarn in the bowl or pot you'll be heating it in later, then cover it with water. Soak the skein for about an hour, to get the air bubbles out of the fiber.

Combine the drink mix powder with water in a small glass or measuring cup. Use about 1 cup of water to one drink mix packet. If you are making several colors during a dye session, keep the colors separate until you are ready to dye. If you don't use all the dye you make, you can store it covered until the next dye session.

Drain the water off the yarn, then pour the mixed dye over the yarn. You can color all of it, adding more water if needed. Or you can pour the dye on only sections of the yarn, leaving some white. If you are using a microwave, place plastic wrap over the bowl and heat it on high for 2 minutes. Turn the bowl, and heat another 2 minutes. Let the skein cool in the bowl before handling.

If you are heating on a stovetop, proceed the same way, but heat the saucepan with the yarn and dye water until it just begins to bubble at a simmer. Remove the pan from the heat and let it cool before handling the yarn.

With either heating method, you'll notice that all the dye has entered the yarn, leaving the water clear. If the water is still colored, reheat to make sure the yarn absorbs all the color.

If you handle the yarn while it's hot, you can burn yourself. Handling hot yarn can also ruin the yarn, causing it to clump or felt, and it will be useless to knit or crochet with later. If you are in a hurry, pour the hot yarn and water into a sink and let it cool there. Once it's cool enough to handle, rinse it in lukewarm water and hang on a clothes hanger to dry.

Slow-Cooker Rainbow

Instead of only one color, you can create a brilliant rainbow effect with this method.

ADULT SUPERVISION REQUIRED

Materials

Slow-cooker pot

Water

Vinegar

Yarn, made from wool or cotton (You can color up to three 4-ounce skeins of yarn if you use a large slow-cooker pot.)

Food coloring (You may need more than the tiny bottles. You can buy large bottles at a restaurant supply store.)

Measuring cup

Plastic squirt bottles (optional)

2 dinner forks or a pair of tongs

Old towel

Clothes hanger

❧ Fill the slow-cooker pot one-third full of water and add 1 cup of vinegar. Put the yarn skeins into the water and add more water until they are just covered. Let the yarn soak at least an hour in the vinegar-water bath. Vinegar is the acid that makes the dye stick to the fiber.

If you are using squirt bottles, fill each half full with water, then add food coloring until it's brightly colored. You'll probably need about 2 teaspoons of food

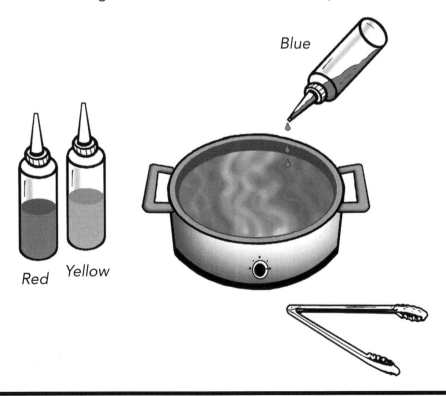

Red   Yellow   Blue

coloring to a cup of water. It might take more yellow than that, so make adjustments as needed.

If you don't plan to use squirt bottles, you can mix the food coloring and water in a measuring cup.

To make a rainbow-type mixture, use squirt bottles of blue, red, and yellow. Without moving the yarn, squirt the colors over three sections across the surface of the water. You'll be amazed at how the colors mix into each other, creating secondary colors. You can use a fork to pull yarn away from the side of the pot, so dye travels down to the bottom, but don't turn or mix the yarn. Let it sit and soak up the colors as they blend themselves into a unique pattern.

Turn the pot on high, put on the lid, and let it heat the dye into the yarn. It will take about an hour. Then turn the pot off, remove the lid, and let it cool. Hours later, you can lift the cooled yarn out with a fork and see the result. You can't predict how the colors will blend, and you can't dye two skeins exactly the same.

The water should be clear if all the dye was taken up by the yarn. Pour out the dye water, and rinse the yarn in cool water. You want to rinse the vinegar out of the yarn, as well as any coloring that didn't stick to the fiber.

Roll the yarn in an old towel to squeeze out the water. Hang it looped over a clothes hanger to dry.

Dye Yarn in a Jar

This is a way to dye several skeins different colors at the same time, because each jar of yarn can be made a different color. If working with a group, each person can have his or her own jar of dyed yarn.

ADULT SUPERVISION REQUIRED

Materials

Yarn—about 100 yards in balls or skeins will fit in each jar. Natural wool or cotton yarn works best, or use T-shirt yarn (see page 138).

1-quart canning jar with lid

Water

Vinegar

Food coloring

Large measuring cup

Microwave oven or stove

Saucepan if using stove

Oven mitts

Clothes hanger

❧ Put the yarn skein in the jar and fill with tap water to cover the yarn. Let it sit for about 20 minutes, until all the tiny air bubbles are out of the yarn. Add water if needed to keep the yarn covered with water.

When the 20 minutes are up, pour out the water, then gently squeeze the yarn to get excess water out. Set the yarn aside.

Fill the jar half full of tap water and add ¼ cup of vinegar. Add drops of food coloring to get the shade you want. Put the lid on and shake the jar to mix. Add the wet yarn,

Cover yarn with water and soak for 20 minutes

pushing it down into the dye. Add more water, or food coloring, if needed.

Do *not* put the lid back on the jar.

If using the microwave, heat the jar on high for 2 minutes. Remove and let cool. Be careful and use oven mitts when removing the jar because it will be very hot.

If using the stove, put the jar in a saucepan and add about 2 inches of water to the pan. Heat to a simmer and continue simmering on low for 2 minutes. Remove pan from the heat and let cool.

Once the dye water is cool, pour it out and rinse the yarn in the sink to remove excess dye and vinegar. Loop it on a hanger to drip dry.

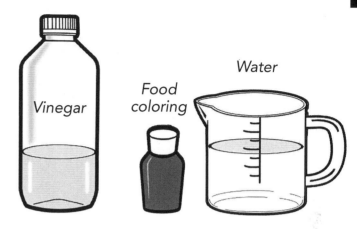

Mix vinegar, food coloring, and water

Add yarn. Simmer in a pan of water for 2 minutes.

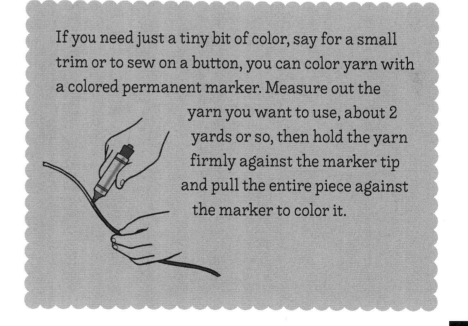

If you need just a tiny bit of color, say for a small trim or to sew on a button, you can color yarn with a colored permanent marker. Measure out the yarn you want to use, about 2 yards or so, then hold the yarn firmly against the marker tip and pull the entire piece against the marker to color it.

Tie-Dyeing

This type of dyeing is not meant to cover the fabric entirely. It's a form of resist dyeing, meaning areas of fabric resist the dye. It can be complex and gives beautiful results. In ancient Rome, people admired imported fabrics from India and China that were colored in unusual patterns. They couldn't figure out how it was done. The secret was tie-dyeing: using string to tie areas of the fabric to make a variety of patterns when dyes were applied. Some fabrics were re-tied and re-dyed up to eight times.

Tie-dyeing today uses rubber bands to squish areas of fabric together so tightly that dye cannot color it entirely. It's an easy skill to learn, and you can color T-shirts, aprons, socks—anything made of cotton fiber. It's great fun because there's no way to make a mistake—the results will usually be surprising.

Materials

Plastic garbage bags or shower curtain to protect work surface
Plastic gloves or sandwich bags on your hands
White cotton T-shirts or other items to dye
Plastic wrap
Rubber bands
Tie-dye kit (includes dyes and plastic squeeze bottles, found in craft stores and craft departments of large variety stores)
Water

❧ Wash the garment first, but don't put it in the dryer—you'll use it wet. The dye will penetrate wet fabric easier than dry.

Protect your workspace by covering it with plastic garbage bags or a plastic shower curtain. Wear plastic gloves to keep your hands from being dyed.

If you're doing a T-shirt and don't want to color both sides at once, slip a piece of plastic wrap inside to keep the dye on the front from seeping onto the back of the garment.

Begin by pinching and twisting sections of fabric, and then sliding rubber bands securely to hold the fabric. The areas

Pinch up the fabric in the center of the shirt

within the twist will stay un-dyed, creating a design. The sunburst effect is the easiest and very interesting. Roll the fabric into a long twist, using three rubber bands to hold it, about 2 inches apart.

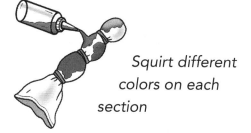

Wrap rubber bands to hold the shirt folds in sections

Squirt different colors on each section

Following the directions that came with the kit, mix the colors. Begin dyeing by squirting the color onto the wet fabric to create designs. Squirt several colors along the roll, leaving a bit of white space between colors to keep them separate if you want. Don't use too much dye or it may run off or move into areas where you don't want it.

When you have finished applying dye, cover the garment with plastic wrap so it won't dry out too quickly. Let it sit for 6 to 8 hours or longer for the dye to set. Follow the directions in the kit for how long to let it sit.

When the dye has set, remove the rubber bands and open up the fabric. You'll be surprised at the patterns you've created. If you're unhappy with how it came out, you can re-tie and dye again while the garment is still damp.

Rinse the dyed garment in warm water until the water runs clear and no more excess dye comes out. Launder the garment

When complete, you'll have a sunburst design

in a washing machine alone or with darker colored garments (in case there's still excess dye left on it). Dry in the dryer.

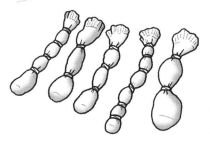

To tie dye socks, roll them up and fasten into sections with rubber bands

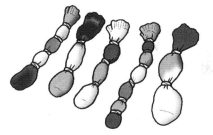

Squirt dye colors on each section

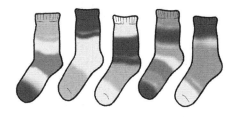

Cool socks!

FREEBIES
Recycled Projects

Once you begin creating fiber crafts you'll begin to see potential project material all around you. If you reuse something, you can save money on buying supplies, plus you can do the Earth a favor by keeping things out of the trash. People outgrow clothes or wear out sheets or other fabrics all the time. Look around at home for these types of materials you can repurpose and ask others to save items for you. Almost any fiber can find its way into one of your projects: old sheets, shopping bags, clothing . . . what else can you think of?

Recycle a Sweater

You can harvest yarn from older sweaters to make new projects. See if you or someone in your family has an old sweater that has been outgrown or has a hole or two. You can also check resale and thrift stores for sweaters made of yarn that is thick enough for your projects. Remember that if the yarn is a light color, you can re-dye it the color you want, following the directions in the dye chapter.

Materials

Sweater (Make sure it is still stretchy and has not shrunk or been felted during laundering, making it impossible to unravel. You should be able to separate the yarn stitches. If they are stuck together, it's been shrunk or felted, and the yarns won't pull apart again.)

Scissors

♣ Look for a sweater that has not been cut and sewn together, or the yarn pieces will be short, as it was made by cutting a flat piece of knitting, then sewing it together.

Look for a sweater that has been stitched together with a knit or crochet yarn chain stitch along the sides and shoulders. Then the sweater will unravel in one long piece. That's because each piece was knitted to shape separately, before it was seamed together.

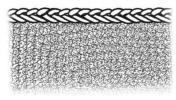

Look for sweaters sewn together like this

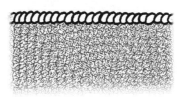

Avoid sweaters sewn together with this kind of stitching

Launder the sweater first. Then turn it inside out and pick apart the seams, beginning at the top of the sweater, pulling the yarn that holds the pieces together. Find the end if possible; you can sometimes get it to pull apart easily. Otherwise, snip away at each stitch.

Take off the collar band, if there is one. Take the sleeves off and unravel them, starting at the shoulder. Start at the neck and unravel down the sweater. Roll the yarn into a ball as you go.

It's hard work to unravel a sweater, but you can gather a lot of yarn that way.

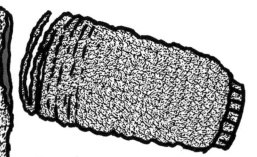

Take off the neck

Begin unraveling at the top of the sweater

Detach the sleeves and unravel them

Make Plarn

Plastic + yarn = plarn, "yarn" made from plastic shopping bags!

There are many ways to recycle plastic, and turning it into a form of fiber is one you can easily do. There are lots of projects you can make with the plarn, or plastic yarn.

Materials

About 30 thin plastic shopping bags
Scissors
Ruler

Cut off the handles and bottom of the bag. Cut strips across both side folds.

❧ Save up at least 30 shopping bags, the thin kind used at grocery stores. To cut each bag into strips, first flatten the bag and smooth it so there aren't any wrinkles. Trim off the handles, then trim off the seam at the bottom of the bag. Cut the bag into strips about 1 inch wide. Cut across the entire bag from fold to fold, cutting through both front and back at the same time. Open the strips and you'll have several loops.

Fasten the loops by tying lark's head knots. Lay one loop over the end of another. Pull one end of the bottom loop over the top loop and then pass it under the other end of the bottom loop. Pull gently to form a knot.

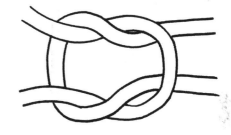

Pull loops through each other to link them

Keep tying on loops. As the plarn strip gets longer, roll it into a ball.

Once you have a ball of plarn about the size of a basketball, you're ready to crochet, knit, or weave it into a project. What can you make? A waterproof soap mat, a scrubby for dishwashing, a tote bag, a mat to put under a pet dish, or a mat to take along to sit on when you're watching a fireworks show. What can you think of?

Plarn Tote Bag

Show this off at the farmers' market, where you can point out your recycling skills while toting a few nice veggies you purchased. It will be about 15 inches wide and 15 inches tall.

Materials

Plarn, about 40 to 50 plastic grocery bags' worth (see page 135)

Large crochet hook, size P or Q (15 mm)

Marker

Scissors

✤ Begin by making a slipknot (see page 19) with the plarn. Working with each loop, you'll crochet with 2 strips of plastic bag at a time. Just let them twist or wrap together as you work. Insert the crochet hook into the slipknot and make a chain 20 stitches long. Make a single-crochet (sc) in the second chain from the hook. Continue making sc stitches in the rest of the chain. When you reach the end of the chain, turn and come back down the other side of the chain. You are making a secure bottom to the tote bag. Continue crocheting in the round, making sc stitches in each stitch, going around and around. Work until the bag is about 12 inches long. Stop working at the end of a row.

With a marker, mark the center of the front and center of the back along the last row you did. Count 3 stitches both directions from that center point, and place another mark. Between these marks will be the handle section.

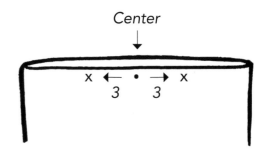

*Mark the handle spot
3 stitches from the center*

From the side where you stopped, begin making sc stitches again, stopping at the first mark for the handle. Don't make a stitch in that handle area; instead make a chain 8 stitches long. Then begin making sc stitches again, starting at the other mark of the handle section and skipping all the stitches between the two marks. Keep going until you come to the handle section on the other side of the bag. Do the same: stop at the first handle mark, make a chain 8 stitches long, then sc stitches starting at the end mark of the handle section.

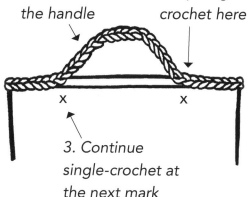

2. Chain 8 for the handle

1. Stop single-crochet here

3. Continue single-crochet at the next mark

Continue crocheting until you come to the chain you made earlier. Make single-crochet stitches on the chain section. Continue crocheting, across both handle

chains, until you are back at the first handle. Cut the plarn about 6 inches from your hook, and pull it into a knot. Tuck the end inside some stitches to hide it.

Charity and church groups crochet plarn mats for people who are homeless or facing natural disasters. People who sleep in sleeping bags can use them to keep their bedding clean and dry. Ask if anyone you know is doing this, then join them to make mats or collect bags for the group. Go online to find a group, or start your own. It takes about 600 shopping bags to make a sleeping mat. You'll help others, and keep the planet clean, with your crochet skills.

T-Shirt Yarn

Simple cotton T-shirts make thick, soft yarn that can be knitted or crocheted into rugs, bags, or mats. It's a bulky yarn, good for thick items that work up quickly with large crochet hooks or knitting needles.

Materials

T-shirts: Soft and stretchy under-shirts are best. They should *not* have seams on the sides.
Scissors
Ruler and pen, if needed

♣ Lay the shirt flat on a table and smooth out all the wrinkles. Cut off the top section just under the sleeves, then cut off the bottom piece just above the hem.

Cut away the sleeve section and hem

You'll have a tube shape from the center section of the shirt. Smooth it flat on the table, then fold it in half. Slide the bottom edge out

from beneath the top edge by about an inch.

Smooth it into a flat tube

Fold in half, with one edge sticking out 1 inch past the other

Cut 1-inch strips across the folded tube from left to right, cutting through the first fold as you start, then cutting across the second fold. Stop there; don't cut into the 1-inch section with the third fold.

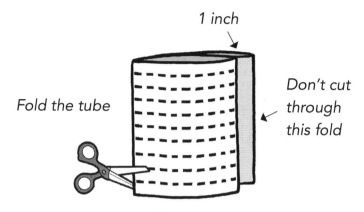

1 inch

Fold the tube

Don't cut through this fold

Cut in strips, cutting through the top fold on the right, but not through the bottom fold

When all strips are cut, open the tube so the uncut section lies faceup down the center. It sort of looks like a backbone and ribs!

Open up the tube with the uncut fold on top

Trim away the first section at the top, cutting on a slant from the first slit down the uncut fold and across to the second cut on the other side. Continue cutting this way, from one side cutting on a slant to the other side. This will result in one long strand of yarn.

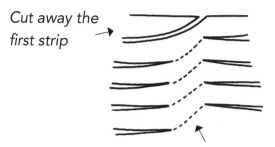

Cut away the first strip

Cut across the spaces between strips on a slant. That will create one long piece of yarn.

If you accidentally cut through the wrong section, just tie that piece on at the end later.

After all the cuts are made you will have one long strip of fabric. Now work gently with both hands to stretch the T-shirt strip. As you stretch, the strip will curl up, rounding its edges smoothly to make a nicer yarn.

Pull the strip to stretch it a bit. It will curl on the edges to make a smooth yarn.

Stretch your way through the entire strip, then roll it into a ball, ready for a project. You can follow the directions for the Plarn Tote Bag, using T-shirt yarn instead of plarn, or make a heavy-duty rug (page 140).

T-Shirt Yarn Rug

It will take at least four adult-size T-shirts to make enough yarn for this project. It will measure about 10 by 18 inches. The more yarn you have, the larger your rug will be. You can make it with what you have on hand, and add more rounds as you make more T-shirt yarn. It can be the rug that's always "growing."

Materials

4 (or more) adult-size T-shirts, made into T-shirt yarn (see page 138)

Crochet hook, size P or Q (15 mm)

Do 2 sc stitches in each corner, every row after row 6

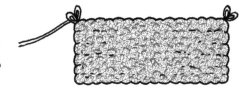

❧ Make a rectangle first. Make a chain 25 stitches long. Turn and begin working single-crochet (sc) starting in the second chain from the hook. Work along the entire chain. When you get to the end, chain 1 for turning. Turn and work sc across the strip. Continue this way for six rows, adding 1 chain at the end of each row for turning, then working sc across. Count your stitches now and then to be sure you keep the same number of stitches.

At the end of the seventh row, begin crocheting all the way around the rectangle. When you get to the end of the eighth row, make 2 sc for the corner, and keep going down the side of the rectangle. You will work in rounds, not rows. Work 2 sc stitches in each corner as you work around the rectangle, so the rug will lie flat. If the rug starts to curl up, begin working 3 sc stitches in each corner.

Making 2 sc stitches at each corner will add 4 stitches each round. That will help it lie flat.

When you run out of yarn, tie on more and keep going. Once the rug is as big as you want, pull the working end of yarn firmly through the last stitch, making a knot. Tuck the end inside stitches to hide it.

Get Involved!

While it's quiet, peaceful, and satisfying to work on your own project, it's nice to work on fiber arts and crafts with others, too. Find a group of friends to knit or crochet with, so you can help each other and have fun showing off your work. Knitting, spinning, crocheting, and weaving groups meet at community centers, libraries, and even cafés, so watch for one to join.

Once you have learned to do a fiber handcraft, you can reach out and teach others. Most people learn to knit, crochet, or spin from someone else. Once you know a few steps, you can be the teacher. Maybe you could start a group yourself!

Each One Teach Two

Once you've learned the basics of knit or crochet, you can spread the happiness. Teach someone else. Better yet, teach two more people. The Craft Yarn Council created a program called Each One Teach Two to help spread the joy of handwork. Visit their website, www.craftyarncouncil.com, for tips on teaching others, easy patterns, and even certificates to show you've learned how to knit or crochet.

Make Things for Others

There are many charity groups that spend time making handmade items for those in need. Some groups knit caps for premature babies to wear to keep their heads warm in the hospital. Some make socks for homeless people and others in need. Some make blankets to send to needy people around the world. There are many ways you can use your skills and talents to help others. Check with your friends and neighbors. They might already be part of a local group creating handmade items to help others. Go online to find national groups, or start one of your own.

Crochet Comfort Dolls

Many people are making comfort dolls to give to children who face abuse or tragedy. Caring crafters have shipped thousands of these little handmade dolls to children around the world: to Haiti after a terrible hurricane, or to AIDS-stricken Africa, or to victims of earthquake devastation. Maybe these comforting little dolls can make those children feel a little better. Because they are made by hand—by someone who cares about them—the dolls are even more special.

You can knit or crochet dolls that are just plain cute very easily, once you know the basic stitches. They are fun to make because each can be an individual, with different hair, skin, and clothing colors. You can use small amounts of yarn left over from other projects. And they are perfect for little children to play with because there are no parts to pull off and swallow. Why not make a few for yourself and friends? Then make a doll for someone else who might need a small comforting doll to remind them they are not alone.

Materials

Yarn, worsted weight, in colors for face, hair/hat, shirt/dress, pants, shoes
Crochet hook, size E (3.5 mm)
Crochet hook, size K (6 mm) for ponytail, if desired
Scissors
Yarn needle
Stuffing, wool or polyester
Black embroidery thread

❖ This pattern will make a doll about 9 inches tall. If you want a larger doll, use a larger crochet hook. You'll make a crocheted tube that will be stuffed and detailed to make the doll. Following are directions to make a girl doll first, then directions for making a boy doll.

Working with the shoe-color yarn, chain 29. Slip stitch into the first chain you made to make a ring. To do that, insert the hook into the first chain you made and pull a loop through both that chain and the one on the hook. Chain 1, then work single-crochet (sc) in the next chain stitch and continue along the chain. Keep going, round and round, working sc stitches into the previous round, in a spiral fashion, until you

143

have made 5 rows of sc in the shoe color.

You'll change yarn colors as you work up the tube. Change yarn to the dress color by tying on a new color, leaving about 3 inches of yarn tail. Cut off the shoe color yarn, leaving a tail. Tuck the yarn tails to the inside of the tube and make 20 rounds of sc with the dress color yarn.

Change yarn to the face color and make 8 rounds of sc.

Change yarn to the hair color and make 8 rounds of sc. Clip the yarn about 12 inches long and pull the end through the last stitch, to make a knot.

Now you have a tube 41 rows long.

Thread a yarn needle with hair color yarn and make loose stitches through the last row of crochet, all around. Pull up the ends tightly, secure with a couple of stitches, then knot and

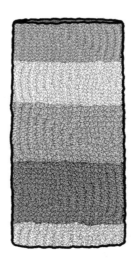

8 rows Hair/Hat

8 rows Face

10 rows Shirt

10 rows Pants

5 rows Shoes

Dress for girl doll

clip the end. Hide the yarn ends inside the hair.

Make the neck: Thread the yarn needle with yarn to match the face color. Make a row of stitches through the bottom row of face-colored stitches, all around the neck. Gently stuff the hair, then the face area. If you push in too much stuffing, stretching the head, it may look too big when you are done.

Pull stitches tight at the top of the head

Pull the neck stitches tight, make 3 stitches to secure the yarn, then clip, knot, and hide the end inside the doll.

Make the feet: Stuff the rest of the body. With matching yarn, sew the feet closed. Then make a few stitches up the center of the foot section to create separate feet. Clip, knot, and hide the end of the yarn.

Stuff the head and pull the neck stitches tight

Make the arms: Using yarn to match the dress, make a row of stitches through the body, going all the way through the stuffing, from the back to the front. Start stitching 2 rows down from the neck, to create a shoulder. End the stitching at the waistline, or almost halfway down the body. The doll will look like its hands are in pockets. Do both arms alike.

Stitch through from back to front to create arms, legs, and feet

Make a ponytail: With hair color yarn and a size K crochet hook, chain 21. Slip stitch into the first chain you made. Chain 20, slip stitch into the same chain stitch as before. Chain 20, slip stitch into the same chain stitch. If you want more chain loops for a thicker pony

tail, make a few more. Cut the working yarn about 12 inches long. Slip it through the last slip stitch to create a knot so the chain won't unravel. Thread the end of the yarn onto a needle and stitch the loops onto the top of the head.

To make a boy doll: The boy can be worked with either hair or a hat. For the hat, you can add a tassel sewn to the top of the head. See page 67 for making a tassel. Follow the directions given for making the girl doll, but after crocheting the feet, crochet 10 rows of sc for the pants. Change yarn, and sc 10 rows for the shirt. Continue using the directions for the girl. After stuffing and stitching the feet, use yarn to match the pants, and stitch a line of stitches from back to front, up the center above the feet, to create legs. Make the row of stitches

about 1 inch long. Pull the yarn tight, then work 3 stitches to hold. Clip the yarn, knot, and hide the end inside the doll.

Stitch on eyes: Use two sewing pins to mark the best spots for the eyes. Push them into position, then slip them out as you begin stitching each eye. Thread a needle with black embroidery thread, doubled and knotted at the end. To hide the knot, insert the needle inside the hat or hair of the doll and push it out at the first eye location. Make 3 stitches for the eye, then insert the needle into the head to come out at the other eye location. Stitch another eye there. Add more embroidery details if you like, such as a nose and mouth, but just two small black oval eyes, stitched with embroidery thread, are nice. If you like, you can add some blusher to the cheeks.

NOTE TO ADULTS:
The Benefits of Fiber Arts

Stimulating our body and senses is central to optimizing our potential, something often overlooked in the current age that emphasizes information and cognitive abilities. Our sense of touch, especially, has been ignored. At times, it's been relegated to the sidelines, as hands-on learning and hobbies are replaced with digital media and screens. My goal with this book is to encourage all of us to use our hands to explore our world and to feel empowered and confident that we can create physical objects with our own fingers.

By working with our hands to transform natural materials, we foster inner growth and a sense of well-being. Handwork brings satisfaction and builds confidence. We learn to slow down and redo poorly done work. Making things with our hands fosters a

social conscience that recognizes wastefulness and respects natural materials. Making something for someone else cultivates altruism. You are consciously thinking about the person, and the anticipation of pleasing someone, which expands into becoming a caring individual.

Fiber arts don't just improve our social and emotional lives, but our mental life as well. By using our hands—our fingers—to explore and manipulate, we stimulate and shape our brain's neurons. Lacking such experiences, our brain simply doesn't reach its potential. Handcrafts develop all regions of the brain: the frontal lobe (attention and planning); parietal lobe (sensory information and spatial skills); occipital lobe (processes visual information); temporal lobe (memory, language, and meaning); and the cerebellum (coordinates precision and timing of movements).

Working with both hands stimulates both sides of the brain. In an activity like knitting or crocheting, one hand initiates and the other supports. They work together, the brain directing both at once, as they act on a spatial object, the yarn. As we work more quickly, the brain establishes a rhythm, linking the left and right lobes. This develops plasticity and efficiency in the brain. The nerve pathways, neurotransmitters, generate impulses back and forth between the brain lobes and the fingers. With repetition, the brain's connections strengthen. Memory is enhanced. Surprisingly, working with our hands stimulates and refines our language arts skills, enhancing our verbal ability. It also releases serotonin, making us feel calmer, more focused, and less stressed.

Handwork is used increasingly in schools to complement curriculum for ADHD students. Whether they create during recess, free time, or as part of class instruction, students are able to keep their hands busy and productive, increasing their ability to focus while ultimately helping them feel accomplishment.

According to Waldorf School curriculum developers David Mitchell and Patricia Livingston, the handwork experience encompasses four phases:

Incubation. We visualize the project, using our imagination. We choose the materials, color, texture, and shape it will become. We recognize that we are about to create something useful and meaningful that others will see, or for a particular person. We begin imagining how it will appear or be received.

Experimentation. We begin the work in sequence, using careful, planned movements. As we see it evolve, we feel free to change it as we see how the project is emerging. Our awareness is heightened as we see the project begin to take shape. We recognize it may or may not be what we had in mind. We are delighted, puzzled, or dismayed. Sometimes we learn what doesn't work, as much as what does.

Reflection. As we generate options in our mind, we make modifications. Mistakes or unplanned outcomes are changed or adapted. We have no fear regarding the outcome—we are in charge of it.

Confidence Develops. The project is complete, and we assess the outcome. Pride and a sense of accomplishment reinforce our sense of self. We are stronger and optimistic about our ability to do it again in the future. We are empowered.

It is never too early—or too late—to energize our brains by taking up humanity's oldest handcrafts, the fiber arts. Work through these fiber arts activities with the young people in your life, then move on to more complicated patterns—or better yet, make up your own designs. After all, what else could generate invention, imagination, problem solving, and altruism?—plus result in something clever to wear!